ENGLAND AND GERMANY

IN THE WAR

Letters to the Department of State

BY

ROBERT J. THOMPSON

American Consul, Aix-la-Chapelle, Germany
(Resigned)

CHAPPLE PUBLISHING COMPANY, LTD.

BOSTON

Dedicated to

THOSE WHO HOLD PRINCIPLE
ABOVE POSITION

TABLE OF CONTENTS

—

PUBLISHERS' PREFACE

THIS book comprises a series of letters addressed to the Secretary of State by Mr. Robert J. Thompson, recently American consul at Aix-la-Chapelle, Germany, who resigned from his post, as the letters explain, purposely to be free from official restrictions in reporting facts of the European war situation as he has found them.*

Mr. Thompson is a citizen of Chicago. He has spent close to ten years in the consular service in Germany and England, and has also spent much time in France, the beautiful Lafayette monument in Paris being the result of his suggestion and effort.

He entered the foreign service upon the recommendation of friends among the business men of the country for the purpose of demonstrating what a successful business man might accomplish in the direction of extending American foreign trade. The character of his reports and observations reveal an independent point of view somewhat out of, if not above the ordinary.

The letters set forth that their author is not pro-German, by predilection or inclination; rather that ties of blood, friendship, sentiment and intimate

---

*["Thompson's Letters" were first printed serially in the Chicago *Tribune*, from February 14 to February 21, 1915. This great newspaper claimed for that period the largest circulation it had had since the beginning of the war, attributing this gain to Mr. Thompson's letters. They created a sensation and much comment.

It is due largely to the demand of the *Tribune* readers that these semi-official despatches extended and elaborated are now produced in book form.]—*Publishers*.

personal relation bind him to England and France; in view of which he submits that his conclusions in favor of Germany were forced upon him directly against his personal inclination.

Of straight English descent, also bearing the high decoration of officer of the Legion of Honor of France, these facts would suggest that he has brought to the study of the situation in Europe an unbiased mind free from all racial prejudice. His interpretation of Germany's position in the war and in the world is from a source not German, but purely American.

The actuating cause of Mr. Thompson's withdrawal from the service was the receipt from the Department of State, on November 5, 1914, of an official instruction ordering him to discontinue certain investigations which he had begun, more particularly in respect to reported acts of cruelty and reprisal, credited to Belgians, Germans and French, upon the scene of war. The official instruction referred to came to him as the response of the government to a letter which he had addressed to the Department of State on September 17, 1914, and which is included in this series of notable letters.

As a sidelight on the character of the author and his activities at Aix-la-Chapelle (Aachen), the western center of German war operations, we reproduce here a tribute from the pen of Mr. James O'Donnell Bennett, staff correspondent of the Chicago *Tribune*:

AACHEN, GERMANY, Jan. 1.—Who is the best friend of the troubled alien, moneyless and all at sea, in northern Germany, these days?

Thompson, from Chicago.

Who deals in the course of one day with the affairs of Germans, Englishmen, Frenchmen, Russians, Swiss, and Japanese, and

Publishers' Preface

at the end of the day has them all looking to him as a kind of international arbiter of individual troubles?

Thompson, from Chicago.

Who escorts a distracted Englishwoman way up to Crefeld that she may visit her relatives, who are prisoners of war there? And who sends her back over the Holland border with tears of gratitude in her eyes for his zeal and for the courtesy of the German officers?

Thompson, from Chicago.

Who gets American correspondents invited to spend a week on the German battlefront in France or at the great headquarters of the German armies?

Thompson, from Chicago.

Who has taken over the work of half a dozen other consuls who have been banished from Germany?

Thompson, from Chicago.

Whether his own country appreciates it or not, the truth is that Robert J. Thompson, American consul at Aachen, has been of more help to more people than any other official American stationed in Germany since the outbreak of the war.

The position of this border city is partly the cause of that; his own willing spirit is the other half of the explanation.

Aachen commands the roads leading into Holland and Belgium and to the great German cities of Cologne and Dusseldorf. It is the headquarters for perplexity and the rallying point for aliens who want to get out of Germany or further into Germany.

Dealing directly with the laconic German authorities, they are likely to receive terse answers or to encounter wearing delays.

Then they turn to Mr. Thompson, and it is Mr. Thompson who alleviates suspicion, smooths away difficulties, and turns rancor into a good understanding.

He can ask much of Germany because the Germans trust him and because they know he never will ask too much.

In fact, he has ceased to be an individual and has become a kind of institution—combination of post office, bank, bureau of inquiry and domestic adviser.

He calms hysterical women and reunites husbands and wives whom the chances of war have widely separated. He telephones and telegraphs until he has got the unsound passports of rattle-brained aliens viséed into some kind of order and authenticity.

He stakes the penniless, seldom with any assurance that he will ever see the color of his money again.

He extricates incompetents and busybodies from troubles into which there was not the slightest excuse for their getting themselves, and at parting he gently impresses upon them that war is war and that the curious American seeking "a bit of adventure" by going into Belgium, would more wisely transfer his operations to Alaska or the Sandwich islands.

He negotiates the checks of persons who placidly wonder why a German hotel keeper will not accept a check on an English bank when the two nations are in a life and death struggle.

He hunts for and finds American correspondents with whom their papers are feverishly trying to get in touch. And he receipts for and forwards batches of letters which come to him halfway across the empire from correspondents in Berlin who cannot otherwise be sure that their papers ever will hear from them.

He gets stuck for cable tolls and he grins.

He reaches the affections of German officers when he goes for automobile benzol, which civilians are not supposed to have, by saying, "It is for the fatherland." Then they choke up and fill the tanks to overflowing.

He forwards gifts sent from foreign lands to prisoners of war in Germany, and to loquacious aliens he says things which cause it to dawn on them that fluency in slander of Germany is no proof of courage.

It is marvelous how he carries water on both shoulders without truckling. Yet the explanation seems to be the simple one that he is patient and on the square. He is tactful without deviousness, and he can be agreeable without recourse to flattery.

Twenty-two years ago Mr. Thompson was a newspaper reporter in Chicago. That was just before the world's fair, and he was working on the old *Times*. There were rumors of dissensions among the fair directors, and the *Times* knew that Thompson, who had been assigned to the world's fair beat, knew the facts.

He acknowledged that he did, but he refused to write the story on the grounds that it would work harm to the whole exposition project. He was discharged.

He says now that no dismissal could have been luckier for

him, for it brought him into relations with many important men and led him into a larger career than newspaper reporting.

Years later he became the father of the project for the presentation of a statue of Lafayette to France by America.

That is why Robert J. Thompson wears in his lapel today the red button of an officer of the Legion of Honor.

In connection with his career as an American consul, the following London dispatch, written by Frederic William Wile of the London *Times*, further emphasizes that the broad life activities of Mr. Thompson are not prescribed by national boundaries.

LONDON, Jan. 9.—Robert J. Thompson, a former Chicago newspaper man, now American consul at Aachen, Germany, while touring the French battlefields recently with members of the German staff, ran across the grave of a French soldier. The marking at the head of the grave bore the name, August Hennocque de Lafayette. The fallen soldier was a direct descendant of the Marquis de Lafayette, who aided the soldiers of the colonies in the American Revolution.

The descendant of Lafayette was the second lieutenant of the Thirteenth French Dragoons, and his body lay buried in a garden near the town of Conflans. The grave of young Lafayette was not discovered by Thompson until four months after he had been slain in battle with the Germans.

Young Lafayette, together with Mr. Thompson's son, Paul, who then was a school boy of Chicago, unveiled the Lafayette monument given to the French republic by the school children of America in 1900.

The father of the slain Lafayette is attached to the general staff of the French army.

Consul Thompson sailed from London today on the liner Transylvania for a sixty days' leave of absence from his post at Aachen. Aachen has been Germany's principal military gateway to the west since the war started.

"Four million troops have passed my door since the war started," Consul Thompson said today.

At no time in the history of civilization have the people of the world, individually, been so intensely absorbed from every angle on any subject as in the causes and progress of the European war.

In spite of racial prejudices, there is a universal and growing demand for fair play, and a desire to get at all the facts from all sides. When the war blaze burst forth on July 31, 1914, Mr. Robert J. Thompson was stationed as American consul at Aix-la-Chapelle, Germany. This was the center around which occurred the initial stirring incidents of military operations. When hostilities opened, every correspondent, and many prominent Americans who were there felt the shock of the war thunderbolt, and insist that Consul Thompson in his work typified the ideal diplomat and American consul. The manner in which he pulled on and off his white gloves in the midst of a group of excited people, while deliberating on this or that question, remaining absolutely neutral and cool-headed, keeping both ears open to the sympathetic appeals of citizens of the nations at war, as well as to the appeal of Americans and other aliens, was an experience that tested his perfect poise. He was master of the situation.

Years of public service and careful observation had prepared him for this very exigency for which he has received the unstinted appreciation of all concerned, including our own state department and other foreign offices. The mere description of his work was praise indeed, dear to an American. He was doing so much and saying so little that a record of those eventful days at Aix-la-Chapelle remains an important chapter in American consular history of international importance.

However much readers may disagree with Mr. Thompson in some of his conclusions, he has a profound and thorough way of presenting his views which are not the result of mere affirmation, but an analysis of cause and effect, and concrete facts and conditions. The powerful and predominant note in these letters, is the practical plan which the author offers for the solution of international problems and the permanent abolishment of war, the one thought uppermost in the mind of all the world today.

In his epistolary discussions there is always apparent an incisive grasp of those vital and essential points that at least modify emotional prejudices if not change convictions. His work impresses readers with the feeling that he is a thinker and that his point of view is based upon personal observations made with painstaking carefulness which recognizes that the most logical conclusion upon any subject must come after a comparative and thorough analysis of events and things clear to the physical vision as well as to academic research.

THE PUBLISHERS.

INTRODUCTION

AMERICAN CONSULATE,
AIX-LA-CHAPELLE, GERMANY.

To the Honorable,
The Secretary of State,
Washington, D. C.

Sir:—

I have the honor to state that, having been accustomed during the years I have spent in the Consular Service, to address the reports of my investigations to the Secretary of State, I purpose now to continue that practice and present herewith the first of a series of open letters, addressed to you, which will contain facts which I have gathered and conclusions which I have reached in relation to Germany and England and the present war.

I feel that I am warranted in following this course for the reason that the facts which I have gathered, and which I shall submit, have been acquired during my long service—practically a decade—as American Consul in the two countries named, including five months' presence at the practical seat of war.

Because of the department's instruction
to make neither investigations nor reports
on the serious—and at that time acute—
subject of military reprisals, I have withheld
all of my observations and reports, until my
resignation would give me freedom to speak
fully and in direct accordance with the facts.

A sense of duty is involved in my action,
as I feel that the atmosphere should be
cleared, and that our fitness to sit at the
great conciliation and arbitration board,
which shall eventually adjudicate the claims
of the contending nations, and shape the
future policy of the world, depends upon our
true understanding of the whole subject—
which can come only through knowledge of
all of the facts of the case.

Having entered the Consular service for
the sole purpose of serving, and not of filling
a soft political job, I sincerely regard my
present action as a continuation of service,
the value of which, I feel, will be enhanced
by the procedure of addressing these letters
to you. They are, as you will note, of a
character supplementary to those already
forwarded to you, from Aix-la-Chapelle,
where the entire series was prepared, in the
line of my duty (as I saw it) as a representative
of the American people on the ground.

My desire is to give testimony in as formal, impartial form as I may be able to submit it—such testimony as history will demand, and sound statesmanship will require.

The modern world is at war. An appalling social cataclysm is enveloping its leading peoples, destroying the lives of hundreds of thousands of them, the most vigorous representatives of the main races of the world, whose loss means a vital subtraction of virility from the whole human race.

To be a witness of this phenomenon—this orgasm of destruction—and to fail to realize its significance, or to apprehend its consequences, and, especially, to fail to investigate and analyze its precedents, would be to fail in my duty—that larger duty which every man owes to his fellows—to society—and which is greater than his duty to himself.

We, who are living at the present time, have a great responsibility, which rests directly upon us—the responsibility of ascertaining the facts behind the great catastrophe that has overwhelmed Europe; and our first need and duty, in this direction, is to lay aside both favoritism and prejudice.

We must be loyal to facts, or we are traitors to life.

The pressure of facts is the real cause of my action in resigning from the Consular service. No other impulse has directed me. I have not been moved to this decision in order to take up my pen in behalf or in defense of Germany. What I shall state will be evidence in behalf of civilization, for sound civilization is what we must have if we are to be rid of war and the causes of war, both desultory and direct.

If what I say of Germany and England may savor of admiration for one and criticism of the other, let me say that my statements will be the result of conviction—of facts which have been impressed upon me and conclusions which have been forced upon me, as a result of years of observation and study, and in spite of an unsympathetic attitude and adverse conclusions previously formed.

Also, if my phrase, at times, may seem extreme or partisan, it is because my convictions having been formed slowly, if not grudgingly, have at last become deep and positive, and thus may color and shape my expression.

It will be my endeavor to interpret, in part, the German people, their motives and achievements, to the American people; to

portray them as I have found them actually
to be, and in this portrayal to show, at least
in a small degree, the part they more recently
have taken in the progress of the world, and
why the success of their institutions and the
potentiality of their national life lead them
to wish to perpetuate both and extend them
as they grow.

If in my report of the conduct of Germany,
leading up to and during the present war,
I submit facts which may be in contradiction
of statements made by others, I do this, not
in a spirit of contention, but in the cause of
justice and progress—to clear away the
accumulation of exaggeration and misrepre-
sentation that now hides the foundation of
truth, upon which all conclusion and action
must be based.

Few will say that Germany has had equal
access with its opponents to the great court
of the sympathy and support of the world.
Especially at the beginning of hostilities,
when all stood aghast, stunned by the stupendous convulsion, instinctively and impul-
sively seeking its cause and source—the
nation to be blamed—more especially at this
crucial time, during these critical first days,
when public opinion was being framed largely
upon the proclamations and representations

of her enemies, was Germany deprived,
utterly, of approach to the public ear.

This fact should not be lost sight of in
estimating the causes of the present state of
public opinion in the United States; and it
affords a reason for those who know Germany
to be different in act and in motive from what
she has been represented to be, to come
forward and state it, and to present and discuss the moving facts of the situation.

But the presentation of Germany's position
in the present war and the revelation of its
aspirations and life are not my ultimate
object in preparing these letters—and especially in addressing them to you. I have
a larger motive than that. In my concluding
letter I shall presume to suggest a line of
action that is open to the United States in
her present unique position, by following which
we may take advantage of our leadership
among nations to effect national disarmament
and forever banish war from the world.

In conclusion, I wish to state that it is
not part of the purpose of these letters to
take direct issue with the attitude of our
government and its administration; not in-
tentionally, at least. I have no personal
quarrel with the Department of State; and
I do not propose to discuss or question the

sincerity of its position or that of President Wilson, who announces his purpose to maintain a strict neutrality.

If the stand of the United States be not impartial in the present desperate international situation, and if your interpretation of the accepted rules of war be unfair, a more definite criticism will be applied to your position and action than any I might assume to make.

I have the honor to be, Sir,

Your obedient servant,

ROBERT J. THOMPSON,
American Consul (Resigned).

ORIGINAL LETTER TO SECRETARY OF STATE

AMERICAN CONSULATE,
AIX-LA-CHAPELLE, GERMANY,
September 17th, 1914.

HON. W. J. BRYAN,
SECRETARY OF STATE,
WASHINGTON, D. C.

Dear Mr. Bryan:—

Events have developed so rapidly since August 3rd, and so continuously, that I no more than find time to write of them before they seem trivial and ancient in comparison with the more recent and important occurrences.

I wish to report to the Department, however, my efforts and their results in the direction of assisting representatives of the American Press to forward important statements to their respective papers and the people of the United States.

On August 29th, John T. McCutcheon and James O'Donnell Bennett, of the Chicago *Tribune;* Irvin S. Cobb of the *Saturday*

Evening Post and Philadelphia *Public Ledger;*
Roger Lewis of the *Associated Press;* and
Harry Hansen of the Chicago *Daily News*,
came upon the consulate, having been conducted by the German military authorities
to Aix-la-Chapelle from the battlefields
along the Belgian-French frontier. The com-
manding officer here declined to issue them
passes to go into Holland or to return to
Belgium, but placed no restrictions upon their
passing further into Germany in the direction of Cologne and Berlin. They elected
to remain in Aix-la-Chapelle, from which
point they could mail articles to their publishers through the nearby frontier-town of
Vaals, Holland.

Their experiences and observations with
and in the rear of the German army in
Belgium, from Brussels to Beaumont, and
from there to Aix-la-Chapelle, covered a
period of ten days and will, before this reaches
you, be published in their respective papers.

On arriving at Aix-la-Chapelle, where the
English and American papers were to be
seen, they were shocked to note the innumer-
able reports of atrocities and brutalities
alleged to have been committed by the
German troops in the territory which they
had just traversed.

These gentlemen, who at the time of their arrival in Europe were decidedly anti-German in sentiment and convictions, at once prepared a joint statement which I advised them I would use my best efforts to have forwarded by wireless to the Western Union Telegraph Company in New York for transmission to their several papers.

Evidently these well-known American journalists were not so much concerned by their desire to send exclusive and startling stories to their papers as they were moved by a sense of fair play for their fellow countrymen, who were entitled at least to a clearer picture of things than they were receiving from an interested source, controlling the sole means of communication between Germany and America. It seemed to me, likewise, most important that the American people have as much of the truth as it is possible to convey to them on the one most terrifying feature of this present war; hence I had their statement telegraphed to Berlin for forwarding by wireless telegraphy to America, if possible.

I have observed that various appeals are being made to America to break its neutrality and join the opponents of Germany on account

of the alleged inhuman conduct of the German
military, its cruelty and drunkenness. I am
here on the frontier where the Belgian
reprisals began and am to some extent
personally familiar with the circumstances
leading to the commencement of these acts.
In a broad sense, it may be said that the
German, and especially the German soldier,
does not get drunk. There are, of course,
exceptions to this rule; but in support of
the military law against supplying soldiers
with alcoholic drinks, the Government has
issued a decree fixing a severe penalty for
soldiers drinking intoxicants as well as for
persons giving intoxicants to them.

There has been a terrific outcry in Germany
against the unexpected participation of the
Belgian civil populace in the war. This
outcry did not arise without definite cause.
On requesting a pass from the Garrison
Commander at Aachen, then General von
Korpff, to send a messenger into a nearby
Belgian village to investigate the shooting
of a British subject, this gentleman related
to me, under great mental stress, instance
after instance of German officers and men
being shot and killed while at rest, by
farmers, even by young girls, whom he
stated fired upon them while passing a

glass of milk or water. He gave me these
details at the moment in order to impress
me with the danger of sending a messenger
into those districts, Baelen-Dolhain, at that
time, August 17th, and his inability to guaran-
tee protection for my messenger.

The reprisals made by the German military
have been severe and possibly beyond modern
precedent, but I am convinced that when the
facts are brought out they will expose causes,
which, under the circumstances, may have
extenuated, if not justified, their conduct,
as the Germans claim.

In Liege I spent the night as guest at the
"Duesseldorfer Lazarett," a temporary war-
hospital, opened August 17th in the main
University building there, by three prominent
ladies of Dusseldorf.

The hospital referred to was attacked on
the 20th of August, three days after it was
opened and thirteen days after the entry of
the German troops into Liege. According to my
examination the building was the object of
rifle volleys from two sides, the effect of the
bullets showing in the broken windows. As
a result of this attack thirteen men, principally
Russian, English and Belgian students, were
caught and executed in the University Square,
and twenty buildings, principally lodging

houses, from whence the shooting came, destroyed.

I hope to be able, if time permits, to investigate certain charges of the murder of sleeping, wounded and defenseless German soldiers, made against the Belgian villagers and farmers just over the frontier between here and Liege.

I will send you, from time to time, some illustrated German papers.

You will pardon this semi-personal letter. I can write more freely in this manner.

With great respects and regards,

ROBERT J. THOMPSON,
American Consul.

RESIGNATION

[*Publishers' Note:* In response to the foregoing letter an instruction was received from the department directing Consul Thompson to cease all investigations and discontinue all reports as suggested—the result of which was the resignation of Mr. Thompson as shown in the following despatch.]

AMERICAN CONSULATE,
AIX-LA-CHAPELLE, GERMANY,
New York, January 20, 1915.

To THE HONORABLE,
THE SECRETARY OF STATE,
WASHINGTON, D. C.

Sir:—

I have the honor to tender herewith my resignation as consul at Aix-la-Chapelle.

"Great stress of work in connection with my position as Consul at Aix-la-Chapelle, both official and of a semi-official nature, has prevented my disposing of the question raised by the Department instruction, ordering me to discontinue investigations and to make no reports on the subject of war reprisals.

"I come now to this matter and if it appear that I have delayed my action, the more important duty of aiding distress and attending to the heart-breaking demands of scores

of applicants of every nationality must be
my excuse.

"A truly neutral person or state can have
neither fear nor favor for the truth, and under
such unparalleled circumstances as those
brought about by the war, a consular officer
who might be stationed at the center of this
great war vortex, will either tighten up on
the technique and formalities of his position,
or go outside of them, to meet in every way
and as best he can, the new conditions and the
pressing demands made upon him. In the
midst of such extraordinary circumstances
no call of duty appeared more definite to me
than that of the keenest observation and
accurate report as to the motives and acts
of the combatants. If a neutral state cannot
separate its belligerent friends and bring
peace between them, it must, I feel, automatically take the position of referee, or
umpire, or sink into obscurity as unequal to
its role as a World Power and an influencing
force upon the wider welfare of mankind.

"There should be no German, French,
Belgian, or English in America at such a
moment as this. There should not be, but
unfortunately there are. We have over
twenty millions of citizens of German blood
in our country, even though their consan-

guinity dates from the days of the colonization
of Pennsylvania, at a time when the English
language was known in that territory only
in official circles. Germanic source or blood
constitutes more than one-fifth of the present
composite body of America, almost one-
fourth against one-eighth or less of English.

"Must the accident of blood and of language
bar these people, with their undying memories
for the Fatherland, from a square deal?
There is no German blood in my veins and
I thank God I am an American, but I
should lose my pride of race if I thought the
American national spirit of fair play were
dead. Even if the operation of international
law, which indicates the rights and duties of
belligerents and neutrals, permit or force us
to become allies of the Allies in the matter of
supplying them with men and vast supplies
of munitions of war; (to say nothing of
reservists, I am advised that some three
thousand of the Canadian troops in England
now are American boys); even if this be
true, which is not denied, it is no less the
duty of the United States to umpire the
game, standing out fearlessly for the exposition of the truth and the administration of
justice.

"In withdrawing from the service at this

time, and under the circumstances, I may
be permitted to state once more and specifi-
cally that I regard it as the special duty and
privilege of a neutral country, through its
representatives and otherwise, in any manner
fairly open to it, to ascertain the truth and
facts in a great human epoch-making event
like the present war; not alone to ascertain
the truth, but to record it for the benefit of
history and the final accounting which must
be rendered to mankind—an accounting
which in all probability must eventually be
made through the mediation of that same
neutral country, conferring upon it the greatest privilege and moral responsibility, perhaps, in the history of nations.

"The instruction seems gratuitous and
trivial in view of the importance of the subject, and the opportunity afforded you, of
having a disinterested bystander on the spot,
who might learn, if not the truth, at least
certain aspects of the truth, concerning the
extreme and appalling charges laid at the
door of a people so intimately and senti-
mentally connected with America as are the
Germans, by others of equal intimate relationship.

"I cannot be alone in the thought that the
most important consideration in our present

national life is to know the truth, and as much of the truth as we can possibly learn on the subject of this war, and first and primarily of its causes and beginnings. If I may be the instrument, even in the smallest degree, of supplying or setting into proper alignment only a few phases of this vast and chaotic panorama in which the hearts and souls of millions of our fellow countrymen are involved, almost equally with the actual participants, my withdrawal from the service for such purpose will indeed be a small sacrifice."

I have the honor to be, Sir,

Your obedient servant,

ROBERT J. THOMPSON,
American Consul (Resigned).

GERMANY'S RISE AND ENGLAND'S DECLINE

AIX–LA–CHAPELLE, GERMANY,
October 29, 1914.

To THE HONORABLE,
THE SECRETARY OF STATE,
WASHINGTON, D. C.

Sir:—

I have the honor to present the following for your consideration.

I think it the duty of every person who feels he can throw light upon the ethics and meaning of the present great war to come forward and speak; and I hope that my observations may be of help to the government in determining its attitude in the future.

For my part I am a great lover of France— the Lafayette monument in Paris, erected upon my initiative, and the high order of the Legion of Honor decoration which has been conferred upon me will attest to that. My blood and ancestry are English. I have lived in France, in England and in Germany. I think my viewpoint is clear and that I am fair and unprejudiced. I suppose it is of little

(33)

importance how I may look at this titanic human convulsion; but I have seen the thing coming on for years, events to which mankind runs forward but which occasion surprise and wonder when they are realized.

You may recall my interview in the Houston *Chronicle* of July 23, 1912, sent to the Department at that time and resulting in my transfer from Germany to Sheffield, England. I repeat it in part, here:—

"Germany is today the most efficient nation, economically, on the globe. Today Germany is second only to England as an exporter of manufactured goods, the United States ranking third. Within five years Germany will pass Great Britain in this respect and lead the nations of the world. The German policy is one of peaceful development of domestic and foreign trade; Germany does not seek offense nor seek occasion to give offense. But Germany is determined henceforth to take a leading position among the world powers in the adjustment of all international issues, and is determined, especially, to press her industrial and commercial development to first rank among the nations, regardless of any opposition which may be aroused by this course in any quarter of the globe.

"When the day comes that Germany passes Great Britain in the exportation of manufactured products, British resentment will perhaps precipitate an armed conflict between these two great nations. The only factor which, in my opinion, may prevent it, is the rapidly increasing socialistic sentiment of both peoples. Socialism stands opposed to war. Great Britain, during the next few years, is going to be socialized to an extent that will virtually revolutionize the British government. The socialists are very numerous and influential in Germany. It is possible, perhaps probable, that the doctrinal opposition to war of the socialists in Germany and Great Britain may prevent the armed conflict toward which so many observers in both countries, and elsewhere throughout the world, have been looking forward fearfully during recent years.

"There is no general wish for war in Germany; war discussion there is confined almost wholly to army officers, who naturally consider a survey of what is ahead as in line with their calling, just as they do in France, Russia, Japan, and other countries. Foreign brokers indulge in some war talk, but the substantial interests of Germany—manufacturing, educational, professional—do not

want war; they deplore the possibility of it,
but will not on that account be deterred
from pressing Germany's claim for pre-
eminence in the peaceful competitions of the
world as rapidly as her people can make
that claim good. Most of the talk of war I
hear in Germany is developed by the war
speculations of newspapers from across the
English Channel."

I have thought that Germany's unchecked
and gradual commercial conquest of England
might in some way affect a revolution of the
industrial classes of England and thus bring
on war, rather than that it would come as
it has. I believe the broad statement may
be made now, in full truth, that Germany,
the youngest nation amongst the great powers,
and even still in infancy—at the commencement of its career—has, to all practical purposes, attained the position of conqueror and
leader of the world from the standpoint of
the present economic ideals and standards of
mankind. I do not think there is the slightest
doubt of this. I have been in one of the greatest typical industrial centers of England for
two years and I have been in the same comparative centers in Germany for six years, and
one would need to be blind, indeed, to fail to
see conclusive evidence of what I state.

In my judgment, Germany has fairly and
definitely won her laurels; and the least
important of her national institutions, in
this respect, is her military establishment,
the thing by which, I think, we falsely judge
her at this moment, when she finds herself
compelled to test its efficiency, to put
it to performance, in holding that which
she has gained through the arts of peace,
and maintaining and preserving it for civilization.

It may be illuminating to take the recent
explanations of the British manufacturing
world for the placing of English orders for
locomotives in Berlin; viz., that their factories, or works, were filled with orders and
they could not, therefore, make delivery in
the time necessary to meet the requirements.
That was the claim. I happen to know the
facts and they are that many of these factories
were not at all fully occupied, at the time.
More particularly, however, all of them were
suffering from arrested development. In
other words, they were operating on the
basis of several decades back, and had not
the initiative to keep abreast of their German
competitors in the way of expansion, as,
according to my observation, is the case with
the English manufacturer generally. The

grandfather's method of doing business there
and of meeting the demands of the world
is no fiction, but a deadening reality.

During the years 1912 and 1913, in many
respects the most prosperous England has
ever experienced, commercially, her emigration was the most pronounced and extensive
in her history. To a very large extent the
English workman had abandoned hope of
any betterment in his own country; and the
continuous desertion of the mother country
by high class mechanics, going to Canada
and the colonies, was growing daily more
and more embarrassing in the way of maintaining efficiency of workmanship. In the
period of Germany's phenomenal advancement in manufacturing and agriculture in
the past thirty years, many millions of acres
of agricultural land in England have reverted
to the sheep range and hunting park. England, who had become dependent upon the
outside world for food, was becoming also
more and more dependent upon Germany
for the manufactured necessities of her com-
plicated and effete civilization—for sugar,
almost exclusively, for chemical products and
dyestuffs used in her great textile industries,
for steel and iron products, and for hundreds
of different kinds of manufactured articles,

which Germany was making better and cheaper than any nation in the world.

Furthermore, England was looking to Germany as an example for her hoped-for rejuvenation and renaissance, even to the extent of seriously discussing copying her financial policy, customs tariff, and her army establishment with the introduction of enforced military service. She had already taken Germany's industrial insurance laws as a model for her own, she was slowly awakening to the wisdom of copying her scheme of technical education. A great movement was afoot to introduce a net work of waterways, similar to that of Germany; and scores of municipal delegations were visiting Germany annually with the view of improving the English cities. The wise men of England saw in all this, and in the rapidly approaching world leadership of Germany in the manufacture and sale of those goods, which, in their production pay wages to workers, an inevitable shift and transfer of the financial center of the world from London to Berlin; and, with the realization of this stupendous fact, came the forecast of the automatic loss, as well, of her place as the political and ethical center of Caucasian civilization.

By the same token that Germany had

fashioned for herself a "big stick," in the
way of her army, to defend herself against
the weed-like growth and threatened expansion of Russia, resulting in her being regarded
as the very apotheosis of militarism, England,
for her own purposes, had also built her
"Big Stick"—her navy—a far greater exhibi-
tion of armament than the German war
machine.

One is in as bad a position as the other
from the standpoint of militarism—excepting
that with Germany we have militarism at
home and efficiency, while with England, it
is militarism of the sea, imperialism and
growing inefficiency.

No people have felt this more keenly than
the English statesmen. They have gravely
realized that the last and only possible
chance for England to retain her position
before the world, politically and economically,
for another generation, lay in the checking of
Germany's progress in the arts of peace. To
meet and pass her in the legitimate operations
of industrial competition was impossible;
they saw plainly that England was hopelessly
outclassed in this field. A way out was found
in the combination with Russia and France,
who were racial antagonists and military
competitors of Germany, and not serious

commercial rivals. By joining these states
in the enterprise of war, England has moved
to regain her position as manufacturer and
banker for the world.

In my judgment, the violation of Belgian
neutrality by Germany as the reason for
England's declaration of war is a sentimental
subterfuge, sounding well for English chivalry
before the world, but meaning, from the
beginning, suicide and death to poor Belgium.
The whole Belgian situation has proved a
fortuitous circumstance for England, the
moral value of which has counted enormously
for her and her allies.

The German, however, is too naive to
resort to this sort of politics, too direct and
simple to lie. He has much to learn, in
diplomacy. Nevertheless, honesty is something, and, in the end, sometimes prevails.

I would not assert that England has will-
fully sought the present favorable moment
for her cause. It came, nevertheless, and
found her as well prepared as she could ever
be, with the combined armies of France and
Russia on her side; and, because of a con-
scious or subconscious knowledge that here
was her final opportunity, it became inevitable
that she should declare war on Germany. I
do not think there was any more possibility

of avoiding this than to prevent a collision
between two locomotives headed for each
other under full speed on the same track.

The merits of the case will rest finally
upon the question as to which is the superior
civilization, that of Germany or that of
England—or better, which offers the most to
mankind. To the American, who judges
modern Germany by the immigrant who
settled in Illinois or Iowa forty or fifty years
ago and did the cobbling and blacksmithing
for the town, the matter is quickly determined, but for those who have witnessed the
phenomenal development of the German
people and nation during the last twenty
years, the thing presents itself in an altogether
different light. And to him who has had the
opportunity to study the conditions in England today in comparison with the conditions
in Germany—economic, moral and political—
as I have had, the question passes out of the
field of academic discussion. The one is
moribund and self-sufficient, the other filled
with the energy of youth, confidence and
hope. A thousand years of English civilization and social endeavor, with perhaps the
best and ablest men in the world at the helm,
arrays an almshouse, pauper-fed spirit against
the highest expression of socialistic co-opera-

tion the world has heretofore known. I will
say, too, that as there is more prosperity,
order, sanitation, and contentment in Germany than there is in England, there is
likewise more liberty and individual freedom
than critics of Germany admit. Men of
sense soon learn that police regulations intended for the comfort and protection of the
citizen are no more an abridgment of one's
liberty than is the rule of the camp that each
man shall fold his own blanket.

By sheer force in numbers of her opponents,
coupled with the unparalleled Navyism of
England, Germany may temporarily lose in
this struggle for her existence and a place in
the sun. But if she does lose, it will be the
same old conquest of conservatism and reac-
tion against the demonstrated progress and
betterment of the world. Sad and unhappy
as the surrender of her position as leader
amongst the organized states of the world
might be for England and to us, it would
come as the result of administrative impotence
and lack of initiative in her adjustment to
the economic and sociological ideals of the
day. By her diplomacy, which has tied her
up with forces passe, on the one hand, and
interests undeveloped and unplumbed, on the
other, she is endeavoring to hold that which,

according to those rules of the game appealing
to fair men, she has truly and fairly lost.

I believe that I am right, and while the
appearances seem to be against Germany at
present, her success, in my judgment, will
sound a great advance in the world of progress
and the enlightenment of mankind.

It is my purpose to send you from time
to time, as I have opportunity to put my
observations into shape, reports on the phases
of Germany's diplomatic encirclement and
isolation, the international crime of surrounding this state, and organizing against her a
combination of hostile forces that spelled
war from its very inception. I shall report
on the much misunderstood subject of German
Culture, of its real significance and importance
to the world; on the matter of German
militarism as against a form of armament far
more dangerous to international peace—a
navyism that demands a standard equal to
that of the two next greatest naval powers of
the world.

It is an easy thing for the American, with
his sporting instinct, to say of England: "I
should like to see her whipped for once."
But this would mean a new and violent shift
in the political status of the world. It would
be like an excision of the vermiform appendix

of civilization, so to speak, which might
easily threaten the life of the patient. For
with the downfall of this age-long leader of
human thought and action the knell of the
Saxon would indeed be sounded. We occupy
no light position. Truth, intellect, science,
progress, and justice, perhaps, in the abstract,
are on the side of Germany, yet, sentiment,
tradition and ethics seem to be with the
Saxon. What I may say or write is not done
with a view to exercising an influence on your
neutrality, it is done in a spirit of full justice,
and, in large degree, against my feelings and
sentimental inclinations.

I see in German dominance a phenomenon
of the great inscrutable Infinite, which, with
the clanking juggernaut wheels of Change
and Progress, advances toward freedom and
light through death and pain and travail.
The compensation to mankind must be salu-
tary, and may be, beyond anything that has
occurred since the crucifixion. I will close
this dispatch by quoting a letter from the
great English historian, Carlyle, written in
1870:

"I believe the Prussians will certainly keep
for Germany what of Elsass and Lorraine is
still German, or can be expected to *re-become*
such, and withal that the whole world cannot

forbid them to do it and that Heaven will not (nor I). Alone of nations Prussia seems still to understand something of the art of governing and of fighting enemies to said art. Germany, from of old, has been the peace-ablest, most pious, and in the end most valiant and terrible of nations. Germany ought to be president of Europe, and will again, it seems, be tried with that office for another five centuries or so."

I have the honor to be, Sir,

Your obedient servant,

Robert J. Thompson,
   American Consul (Resigned).

DIPLOMACY'S ISOLATION OF GERMANY

AMERICAN CONSULATE,
AIX-LA-CHAPELLE, GERMANY.

THE HONORABLE,
THE SECRETARY OF STATE,
WASHINGTON, D. C.

Sir:—

I have the honor to present the following brief analysis of the enforced diplomatic isolation of Germany and her encirclement by a combined military establishment four times greater in magnitude than her own:

When Kaiser Wilhelm sent his famous telegram to President Kruger of the Boer republic, I believe the present war was forecast, if not assured. This is the telegram: "I express my sincere congratulations that, supported by your people, and without appealing for the help of friendly Powers, you have succeeded, by your own energetic action, against armed bands which invaded your country as disturbers of the peace, and have thus been enabled to restore peace and safeguard the independence of the country from attack from outside." That was in 1896. When the Boer War came on shortly after, King Edward found the French crying, "Vive Kruger!" "To death with the English!" "A mort and a bas l'Edouard!" and the same sentiment more or less in Germany, more, in fact, as Germany was growing and France was marking time. These conditions convinced Edward that the "Splendid Isolation" policy of Salisbury might be surrendered for a while, and he chose the Kaiser as his successor in this role. England's isolation, however, was voluntary. The present isolation of Germany was forced upon her through diplomatic strategy, designated by the Germans, conspiracy.

England's mastery of the diplomatic world is historic. It is confirmed by the present line-up of the European powers against Germany—accomplished, as leading Englishmen assert, at some sacrifice of soul and future serenity. The English do not close their eyes to the incongruity of their strange compact with Russia, nor to their unique alliance with France—both nations her ancient and classic enemies. The formation of this alien combination by the emissaries of Edward VII— the consummation of this unprecedented

diplomatic trade—really precipitated what
it was intended to guard against, for the
antagonistic impulse created by it led directly
to the opening of hostilities in the Armageddon
raging the world today, and which threatens
to destroy civilization before it is finished.

What was the direct and inevitable result
of the combination? To check the growth,
by minimizing the power, of a vigorous and
successful commercial rival. To encompass
Germany from two sides, and patrol it from
the offing. How does England expect to
close the account with Russia, Japan and
France in case she is victorious? Suppose
Japan demands the further reward for her
participation in this affair, of Hong Kong,
and Russia lays her hands on Persia and
India. Germany's defeat, as well as her
success, is likely to spell disaster for England.

It is not the militarism of Germany that
is the cause of the war. On the contrary, it
is the diplomacy of Lord Lansdowne and
Delcasse in operation, the working out of
their compact to put the lid on and check a
great and progressive rival—a people whose
success, whose marvelous development and
unparalleled advancement, is due to plodding,
industrious effort, to new and up-to-date
adaptations of their social forces to the present

day economic ideals of mankind. To mislead
the world, to deceive herself, in fact, England
has brought into the premise of this possibly
last chapter of her greatness the justification
of militarism, autocracy and the violation of
Belgian neutrality. She would present a nobler
figure to the world if she would tell the truth.

It is a peculiar philosophy that will con-
demn efficiency, be it either in the making of
cotton goods or cannon. If the German
army is accredited with being the best in the
world, it must be charged to those Teutonic
qualities which have also counted for so
much of the world's progress in the pursuits
of peace, and not in any sense to a military
spirit.

Germany is said to have led in the prepara-
tion for war. This is hardly true. Russia's
standing army in times of peace is more than
double that of Germany's in numbers; that
is, 1,500,000 men against 672,000.* Her annual military budget exceeds Germany's by
$36,000,000. But that is not all. Menacing
her on the front, or, at least, if not menac-
ing her, existing just the same, stood France
with an army of 620,000 men, and an army
of 620,000 for France, with her population of
40,000,000 souls, is equivalent to an army of

---

* Data in this chapter is all taken from Whitaker's Almanac, London, 1915.

1,085,000 men for Germany. In other words, the military establishment of France alone, population for population, is quite 40 per cent greater than that of Germany.

We neutrals should try to be fair, and not be governed by our prejudices and senti- ments. We cannot close our eyes to facts. Russia, with a peace footing army more than 100 per cent larger than that of the Kaiser's, on the one hand, and France with a peace footing army 40 per cent (in proportion to population) greater on the other, both avowed racial and military competitors of the German, made it the duty of the Kaiser, and undoubt- edly his very highest duty, to prepare, and hold himself always prepared for the impend- ing, if not inevitable assault.

I can see it in no other light than that this was Germany's contract to civilization, to preserve herself, her nationality and her culture against the combination of Russia and France, and a big enough contract it was. She was in a most heroic position before the war, facing front and back the combined peace footing armies of Russia and France of 2,100,000 men—three to one against her 672,000 men. It will be seen that with one- third the number of men and half the money she has succeeded in maintaining the peace

of central Europe for a period of forty-five
years.

So there you have the situation—the big
and simple analysis of the German militarism,
"mailed fist" and "war lordism," which we
have heard so much about. I give peace
footing figures only, here, as all others are
speculative and uncertain. I have already,
in a previous connection, directed attention
to the fact that the American regular army,
which is one-tenth the size of Germany's,
costs us to maintain it just an even one-half
the amount that Germany spends on her
whole army establishment. While the American people have neither sympathy nor much
respect for militarism, at home or abroad,
they will, nevertheless, agree that Germany
would have presented the aspect of a poltroon
had she not done exactly what she has done,
or even more.

It is probable, judging from the past forty-
five years, that Germany, of all the great
powers, the only one to keep the peace—
the only nation that has not been at war—
would have been able to maintain this condition indefinitely and pursue her destiny in
comparative quietude and neighborliness with
France and Russia, had continental Europe
been left alone. But along about 1898,

English diplomacy, in the form of "Balance of Power," "Sphere of Influence," "Holding His Own," appears in Paris and Petersburg, and the isolation of Germany is underwritten and sealed—fixed and financed. Shortly, the Kaiser sees this vast encircling force, this formidable and hostile coalescence, taking on another 160,000 men of arms and an additional annual war fund against him of $150,000,000. It has seemed to men like myself, and to American army officers who have spent a year or two at such places as Hanover and Berlin, that whatever might happen, Germany could, after all, defend herself, against the whole of Europe. Neither Italy nor Austria count for much in this great line-up of forces. Austria has her hands full with the Balkans and Italy has, so far, stayed out of it.

Now why this isolation and smothering policy of England against Germany? Wars don't begin with the firing of the first gun; murder is not committed on the spot. Both must have their causes, their premeditations and preparations. They spring from and course along psychological grounds. When this entente had been adjusted by the diplomatic cabinets of London, Paris and St. Petersburg, against the German Michael,

and a standing peace footing army of
2,260,000 men in Russia, France and England
surrounded him, English diplomacy returned
to its island home and awaited results.

Right here, I think, is where it was incumbent upon England to fling out a declaration to the world that she would be no party
to the protection of Servia from what many
people consider to be a just and proper
punishment or, if her underwriting with
the Czar made this impossible, then the
contrary, that she would fight, too, if Germany went to war with her continental
partners. Unfortunately, she did neither.
Russia and France knew that England must
fight and that she had dickered with them
for this very occasion. It is my belief that
time and history will place the blame for the
war right here, on the English alliance with
Russia. England refused—she could not
give the assurance to Germany that she
would keep out of the war if the neutrality
of Belgium was respected. In his dispatch
to Ambassador Goshen, at Berlin, August 1st,
Sir Edward Grey said he could not give
Germany the promise that England would
remain neutral on that condition alone—and
on August 4th, to Sir Francis Villiers, his
British Majesty's minister to Brussels, a

peremptory order was communicated to the
Belgian government in which England de-
manded (expected) that Belgium would resist
by any means in its power the demand of
Germany to cross her frontiers, and that his
British Majesty's government would support
it in such resistance.

So we have poor Belgium between the
devil and the deep sea; facing a dilemma
which could be solved only by her sympathies
and prejudices. Belgium is an abomination
of desolation. From the points where the
promised support of England and France
met the German advance—say at Dinant and
in Flanders—it is a nauseating nothingness.
Where the support was not in evidence she
still breathes, where it was given there is
death. And still the Belgians wait daily in
Brussels and the villages for the coming of the
English—for the entry of the French and
Russians. But I do not think, even while
we weep for Belgium, and stand aghast over
her condition, the two and a quarter millions
of armed and trained soldiers, the bristling
circle of steel, placed around the frontiers of
Germany as the result of the supposedly
clever work of Lord Lansdowne and his
diplomatic confreres, Delcasse and Cambon,
should be forgotten. That was the monster

blunder of modern diplomacy. Poor France, once again her sons bleed and die for the ambitions of little men.

Here you have four great powers of Europe fighting for world leadership, to which they think they are all entitled. Russia should wait—her time will come. France must be satisfied, for her day is past. But for England, still the able and clever diplomatic leader of the nations, the fight is hers. Her instruments are the mythical "Balance of Power," "Spheres of Influence," and "Isolation" of her competitor.

It would take seventy years for Germany to become as thickly settled as Belgium, with her normal increase of population, and several decades to reach the same ratio as Holland. The assumption that she needs additional territory for her sons and daughters is an error. Her increase in population, as a matter of fact, does not keep pace with her progress in industry, by nearly 100 per cent. It is a punishable offense to preach emigration in Germany. (Our American Mormon missionaries will testify to this.) Furthermore, she herself, under official control, assists the temporary annual immigration to her fields, mines and public works, of not less than a million laborers—from the provinces of Russia

and from Italy. In addition to this, three million female German workers are engaged in her
fields and gardens during the summer months.
With her intensive agriculture, her tremendous
industrial demands, she could absorb the
entire population of England, and then be
no more thickly populated than Holland;
and if she took, in addition to this, the
population of France, she would have but
about the same number of inhabitants to
the square mile as Belgium. Let the legend
that Germany requires, must have, more
room for her increasing people, be dismissed.
That is buncombe and belongs to the Balance
of Power series of unfounded assumptions.
Statistics prove that Germany requires immigrants not emigrants. She was *isolated* by
her neighbors, not because of a fear of her
ambition for physical expansion, but because
her new spirit of nationalism compelled her
to take a political position as a World Power,
in accordance with her undisputed champion-
ship in the real pursuits of modern life:
science, economics, education and social and
civic progress; and right here is where it
seems to me the miscalculation of Germany's
opponents has been made, and where they
will fail, even as the church failed to suppress
and isolate Martin Luther, and the slavery

sentiment of America miscarried in its efforts to
bottle the abolitionists and Abraham Lincoln.

The misconception of the real movement
in Germany is astonishing. The thought has
grown up throughout the world that the
Kaiser, with a standing army of little more
than a quarter the size of that of those
cordialled against him, has been dreaming of
going out to annex the rest of Europe. Germany's dreams of conquest were in the
humanitarian fields of commerce, of applied
sciences and beautiful cities, of transportation
and the liberal arts; and if she is to be beaten
down, the real spoliation of the war will be
here, and not over the face of Belgium, nor
in France, nor in Poland, nor even in Sussex,
Surrey or the West Riding of Yorkshire.
Whatever happens in these places can have
no final effect upon the result, because Germany's chief progress is an intellectual one,
and something that is impossible of isolation,
blockade or bayonet charge.

Germany turns out the biggest ocean liner,
two, three, of them. England builds the
biggest battleship—dreadnaught. The policy
of German isolation must extend to the sea
as well as the land. Germany's foreign trade
increases and approaches that of England at
terrific speed. She controls the markets of

South America, of the near and far East.
She competes successfully with England in
Sheffield, Manchester and London; and as
her foreign trade assumes a magnitude certain
soon to surpass that of her island rival she
rushes her naval construction, also, corres-
pondingly. Now, who was really prepared
for this war? England, with the combined
navies of France, Russia, Japan, and a peace
footing army of 2,260,000 men at her com-
mand, or Germany, with her regular army of
672,000 men, her untried navy and her obli-
gations to hard-pressed Austria on her hands?
Here you have what we may call the diplomatic layout of the war game, its actual
frame-up. But I think the combination will
fail because of its miscalculation of the spirit
of the German people. Truly there is but
one thing that would precipitate a revolution
or uprising in Germany—one thing only—
and that would be a weakening of the Emperor
or government in the matter of defense or
prosecution of the war. Let there be no
mistake, Germany certainly will not grow
weary. If the world ever witnessed an
example of the spirit of all for one and one
for all in action, it may see it now in the
people of the imperial, confederated states of
the German nation.

The cause of the war then, might justly be
laid at the feet of Lord Lansdowne, Edward
VII, Paul Cambon and M. Delcasse, with
Sir Edward Grey, that astute and masterly
head of the British Foreign Office and diplomatic leader of the world, as regisseur of the
performance. Isolation, that was the plan.
To place Germany by herself. To keep her in
the shade—out of the sun of international
politics. To turn the world loose upon her,
through manufactured alarm and misdirected
hatred. This arrangement to either suppress
or destroy the one nation which has become
a model of civic and social advancement,
should be exposed and understood, and if it
is, the American people will not hesitate to
level the finger of admonition at England
and France for their part in it.

I say all of this with reluctance and morti-
fication, for I love both England and France.
I believe they are engaged in a hopeless,
if not, indeed, a wicked cause, measured
both by the sacrifice and woes they bring
upon themselves, and their effort to check
the progress of the world by laying low its
chief and most brilliant exponent.

I have wept with the mothers and wives
of the best young blood of England. I have
searched the battlefields for the torn bodies

of cultured and beloved scions of the first families of France, even to the descendant of our beloved Lafayette. I have aided in the recovery of the wrecked remains of lost and killed sons of the Fatherland, and with all my love of France, my attachments to England, I must confess I could only see in it all the fruition of the *diplomatic* scheme of enforced German isolation, which could only be likened to an imbecile undertaking to control the tides of the sea or the lightning flashes of the firmament.

I regard the endeavor to isolate Germany, effectually, to be as futile as an attempt to place the lid upon Vesuvius.

I have the honor to be, Sir,

Your obedient servant,

ROBERT J. THOMPSON,
American Consul (Resigned).

SEA VS. LAND MILITARISM

AMERICAN CONSULATE,
AIX–LA–CHAPELLE, GERMANY.

To the Honorable,
THE SECRETARY OF STATE,
WASHINGTON, D. C.

Sir:—

I have the honor to submit the following facts and comments upon the subject of militarism of the sea and land, as expressed in the respective armaments of England and Germany:

Over six million acres of our cotton lands are put out of commission as a first material tribute to "militarism"—but militarism of the sea—which has closed the market for some three million bales of our standard southern crop. Our second tribute is a matter of $70,000,000 worth of copper, $25,000,000 worth of lard, and a score of other things which our good people raise or coax from the earth, to exchange for German chemicals, dye stuffs, toys, cloths, paper, glass, etc. Our export trade to Germany, Austria and Russia, now practically cut off from our markets

(63)

through militarism—of the sea principally—
is a matter of some seven hundred million
dollars.

England, the chief exponent of militarism
of the sea, had ready and building, at the
commencement of the war, six hundred and
seventy-eight war vessels. Her expenditures
for 1914–15 were to amount to $257,750,000,
as a militarist-naval tax on the people of
Great Britain, required for the maintenance
of the Royal Navy. The guns of the Queen
Elizabeth super-dreadnaught fire a projectile
of 1,950 pounds, and a broadside is a mere
matter of eight tons of solid steel. The
personnel of the British Navy is 151,000 men.
It was this form of militarism that tore
Copenhagen and Alexandria to pieces—that
bombarded and burned our own Capitol and
Congressional Library, at Washington. It
is the Royal British Navy that made the
subjugation of neutral and smaller states
and peoples, all over the world, a fact. England's greatness is synonymous with the
supremacy of her navy; and its greatness and
efficiency, no doubt, have saved her many a
war. It is a fighting machine pure and
simple. It was created for the purpose of
attack, essentially. It is not what one would
designate as the sword of defense of the

gentleman, but the weapon of the aggressor and super-power.

I know that the personnel of the navies of the world, and that of England, especially, combine the finest, bravest, and most honorable men in existence. But, as between militarism of the sea and militarism of the land, the least formidable and dangerous to peace, if not the most romantic, is the latter. The one is an away-from-home, interfering, intimidating and marauding affair, the other is a hearthstone, home defense institution.

Being, like yourself, Mr. Secretary, neither a military man nor a naval expert, it seems to me this is a fair, unprejudiced view of the matter. There has always been as great an activity amongst the arms and armament makers of Birmingham and Sheffield, as there has at Essen, or Liege. In this respect there has been no difference excepting that a slab of armour plate or a 15-inch naval gun never looks as dangerous as a Liege pistol, a Colt's revolver, or a machine gun.

I am convinced that the objection of the American people to the so-called German militarism is not to the thing itself, but to its earnestness and efficiency, the undoubted business-like aspect of the German army in times of peace, to say nothing of it when the nation is armed. But the German army, like the German transatlantic liners, German chemical works, German technical schools, German science, German industrial insurance, German municipal government, or German anything, excepting diplomacy, would not be the German army at all if it did not take itself seriously and strive for perfection there as well as elsewhere. Thoroughness is the one prime German characteristic, and though these people might have the best of everything else in the world and not excite fear and distrust, so soon as the world realizes or thinks the German excels in its war installation, it cries militarism, mailed fist, autocracy, and indulges in a lot of other epithets which mean nothing at all more than that it is willing to be beaten in all the genuinely big things of life, but in this it doesn't want to play.

America has regarded the German regular army from the only standpoint it could judge any standing army, that is, from a comparative point of view, from the troops at Fort Sheridan, Fort Leavenworth, or the Texas frontier—a group of outcasts, half criminals, and ne'er-do-wells. This is wrong. The German army is nothing more than a per-

fected militia—the soldiers are citizen soldiers.
Instead of serving two weeks a year in the
field, and one or two nights a week in the
army, they serve one or two years, as the case
may be, and then return to their civil occu-
pations, their places being filled by new men
from year to year, as the youth of Germany
comes to military age.

In a previous letter I stated that the
German military establishment was one of
the least important expressions of its national
life. This is not quite true, because its army
is essentially its Sandow, jiu-jitsu, morning
exercise scheme. It was old Friedrich Ludwig
Jahn, the father of the Turners, to whom a
statue stands in the city of Freiburg, who
met the German spirit for regimented physical
exercise sixty or seventy years ago, and
organized the great Turner Bund. Von
Moltke, Bismarck and Kaiser Wilhelm I
used that spirit out of which to create the
German army. It was originally figured out
as a plan to bring forth a superior physical
race. In the present utilitarian age this
necessity for co-operated effort in the German
character, even in the most excellent practice
of physical culture, became the soul and
spirit of the imperial German army. So,
as you yourself have seen, the youth of

Germany, sons of the idle rich as well as the
unidle rich, princes of the royal families
as well as the yokels of the field, all but
criminals (who automatically lose their rights
to enter the army) and inefficients, have been
regimented and trained to march, to sing,
to play, to put the shot, to do the Marathon
and goose step, to rise in the morning at six
o'clock and get to bed at ten, to get off into
the fields and sunshine, and dig in the sand,
to swim, to jump, to ride, to eat wholesome
food, to keep clean, and to obey, to work
together as one man, and incidentally learn
to shoot. This has been the Kaiser's crime,
that is the militarism you have been afraid
of; and do you know that this splendid and
effective school of German manhood and
efficiency, of health and virility, has cost the
German nation just once again the price of
maintaining our American army, which contains but one-tenth the number of men
enrolled in the peace footing army of Germany? (See Whitaker's Almanac, 1915,
page 105).

During my seven and a half years of
service as consul, in Germany, I have been
a butt for inquiry from hundreds of pros-
pective emigrants to America, Canada and
Brazil. In this time I have never known

personally, nor have I ever heard of a single instance of a young German wishing to leave his country to avoid military service. I have personally known hundreds who have striven to pass their gymnasium or high school examinations in order to limit their period of service to one year. Military service has accomplished this for Germany, in addition to improving its health and efficiency: it has implanted into the minds of its citizens a sense of duty to the state quite inconceivable to the American or British mind—it has made a living reality of the motto of the Prince of Wales: "*Ich dien.*" This, of course, is the modern Germany you have heard of. What it was prior to 1870, when it was composed of a score or more of fusty sleepy kingdoms and principalities, and what I believe the Allies think it should be now, is quite a different thing. "I serve," is the spirit of Germany today, in peace, and it is more than that in war—it is a fetish. And the greatest servant of all is the Kaiser, typifying in his character, more than all else he has been charged or accredited with, the spirit and ideals of the nation. This is the mysterious spirit of the Hive, the Zeitgeist, and national transcendentalism of the German people. Call it

militarism, humanism, barbarism or what
not, in my judgment it is and has been for
the past twenty years the one great and
promising phenomenon of civilization, the
shining hope and assurance of progress of
mankind.

England has set herself the task of crushing
German militarism, of redeeming christianity
and Russianizing Eastern Europe. Association with the German individual or with a
detached group of German individuals would
make it seem possible, if not easy. But I am
afraid England does not fully appreciate the
contract she has taken on. Her militarism
of the sea should protect her great foreign
trade and make her secure in her colonies,
barring, of course, the possibility of her
eventual defeat by the Germans at sea. A
full and complete victory of German arms in
Europe, and even in England, would leave
the naval question unsettled, because the
British Empire would still be at home in
Canada, in Australia or in India, and it
could raid the commerce of the conqueror
from the various bases, for an indefinite
period. Thus would be brought home to
the world the real importance and fatal
significance of militarism of the sea, an
instrument infinitely more opposed to inter-

national peace than any strictly military
organization could be.

But Germany did not purpose remaining
at home, either. One of her new national
expressions was that of international industrial and economic supremacy. A few
years only would have seen her the mistress
of the world in the matter of foreign trade
and merchant marine. This was an inevitable
fact and it was this that forced the rushing
of her naval construction program—to be
in a position to protect her enormous and
preponderating commerce against her defeated
commercial rivals. England has looked with
contempt, distrust and indignation upon Germany for her seeming effort to compete with
her for the position of policeman of the sea,
and every new German battleship has raised
the war scare in England and fixed the
determination there, faster than ever, to
"Hold Her Own." She would surrender the
palm to Germany in industrial, economic and
civic rivalry, but she would not part with
the trident. That, like the Church of
England, had been given by Henry VIII,
and was as sacred as her money system, her
weights and measures and her atrocious land
ownership scheme.

This purpose to remain the master of the

sea, is all very well and noble enough. It
has been the one great saving ambition of
Britain, but it is not for her to cry "Mailed
Fist," "Militarism," and all those fearful
sounding things to the good reason and fair
play sentiment of the world. If we agree with
the claim that England and her supreme militarism of the sea stand for the restoration of
Christianity, the suppression of vandalism,
the crushing of Germany, very well—but as
neutrals in this terrific cyclone of horror,
we must get our proper bearings and render
justice, so far as it comes to us to do so, to
all sides.

Militarism of the sea means suppression
of commerce in time of war. It means the
suppression of our commerce. It means
millions of suffering workers in the south.
It means unemployment for hundreds of
thousands of non-combatants all over the
world. It is a part of war and it is fair, the
least cruel of all forms of warfare, perhaps,
because the widest in its effect. Whether we
will or no, it forces the co-operation of every
neutral in the world. It makes us allies of
the big tonnage, right or wrong. It is the
real big stick Mr. Roosevelt was wont to
talk about so much. If America sees war
ahead with Japan, England or Germany, let

her go to the navy program. No nation can
fight and upset the world without a navy,
but it is a certainty, if the present war results
in disarmament, and that is another moral
obligation England has taken on, the dreadnaughts and submarines, the sea mines and
torpedoes, will assuredly be the first to go to
the scrap heap. Then what will become of
India, of Egypt, of South Africa, and the
new Cyprus? What will become of our
own imperialism, the Philippines? Militarism
from the Teutonic standpoint subjugates no
people. Nor would the militarism of France
or Russia have brought on the war had it
not been for the big tonnage of England.
Even with their vastly superior forces they
would never have undertaken it, and Germany, having everything to lose, and not
so much as the value of a single man to gain
on the continent of Europe, would have
certainly avoided it.

This is the situation, as I see it. The
Kaiser worked always with the idea that with
the best, if not the biggest, "big stick" in
the arena of European military rivalry, he
could maintain the peace, and for twenty-
five years he succeeded in doing so, and now
the glove is on the floor and the German
nation is battling to save and prove the

efficiency of her wonderful culture to the
world. Success or failure for her means
international political leadership on the one
hand, or practical destruction on the other.
It means advance or stagnation. It means
that Russian, French or English civilization,
statecraft, shall be the standard of intra-
social ideals and human welfare for the next
hundred years, or so. It means that and
nothing else. The atrocity business, "baby
killing," "militarism," "navyism," "the
Kaiser," "scraps of paper," and all the other
cries of the Powers, do not enter into the
merits of the contest in the slightest degree.
They are mere incidents of something so
vastly more important to us that they will
be forgotten in the great onrush of events to
the goal toward which mankind is inevitably
and irresistibly driven. Let us get beyond
the diverting incidentals to the main issue.

England would make this our fight as well
as hers. In fact, with her control of the sea,
we automatically become one of her principal
allies. She would make us a party to the
attempted isolation of Germany. She would
have us commit ourselves to militarism of the
sea as against militarism of the land; she
would have us join her in her effort to turn
back the clock of destiny, and aid her in

retaining the pennant of leadership which is slipping from her mast. We have no naval competition with England; ours would be with Japan, if with any power, and, besides, we have a goodly hostage both for her respect of the Monroe Doctrine and for her general good behavior in Canada. But the mysteries of the foreign office of England are wide and deep. Supposing they disclosed an alliance with the sons of the Mikado against us in case of war with Japan?

We witnessed a year ago a combination of the British and German governments to the disadvantage of our Exposition at San Francisco, much to our surprise and chagrin. Just now this is a very sore point with the German foreign office. For they were told by England: "stay with us in this matter and we will bring about a readjustment of the Panama Canal tolls." Perhaps the Hay-Pauncefote scrap of paper would be patched together. And it was so, much to our credit. But the militarism of Japan, the militarism of England, or of the Kaiser, could no more affect us than the militarism of Russia, without the introduction of militarism of the sea. Germany and England were much more intimately connected before the war than is the United States and England. England was Germany's best customer, and Germany was England's best customer, in trade. They are connected by ties of blood relationship, marriage, quick transportation and a thousand industrial interests, and yet England turned her naval ally, Japan, loose upon Germany in the Pacific.

So, in this moral support and sympathy business—and God forbid we should go any further—it behooves the American people not to be carried away by every clap trap, holier than thou talk, on the part of any one of the belligerents, of England, Germany, France or Russia. None of them wanted the war—unless it was Austria in her purpose to punish the assassins of her Archduke, and Russia, in her thousand year ambition to expand to the south and west, finding her opportunity in a powerful combination with France and England against Europe's one bulwark against her encroachment— Germany.

Let us give the Kaiser and so-called German militarism a square deal. If we are to umpire the game, let us, at least, balance our prejudices and sympathies and keep an open mind. Militarism is militarism, whether on land or sea. If part goes all must go. And in the great world family of nations, secret or open, offensive and defensive, alliances should be regarded as an international crime.

I have the honor to be, Sir,

Your obedient servant,

ROBERT J. THOMPSON,
American Consul (Resigned).

CERTAIN ASPECTS OF GERMAN CULTURE

AMERICAN CONSULATE,
AIX–LA–CHAPELLE, GERMANY.

To THE HONORABLE,
    THE SECRETARY OF STATE,
        WASHINGTON, D. C.

Sir:—

I have the honor to submit the following observations on certain points and phases of the present somewhat mooted question of German culture:

The hard sound of C does not exist in the German language. Its letters have only one sound and words are pronounced as they are spelled. A spade is called a spade in Germany—a thimble is a hat for the finger, or *Fingerhut*, and a telephone is a far-speaker, or *Fernsprecher*. So, very naturally, in this land of fiction, fable and song, and above all, of truth, culture could be nothing else than *Kultur*. It is not likely that the world will lapse into complete forgetfulness of the invention of printing at Mainz by Gutenberg, a

science which is at once the foundation and
sub-structure of all permanent culture of
the modern world, and so essential to the
moral campaign now waging against the sons
of Teuton—"the baby killers," as Mr.
Churchill has so facetiously dubbed them.
I think that gentleman must have forgotten
his kindergarten, a bit of German "Kultur."
He forgot, or did not know that the children
of England were crying for German toys this
Christmastide—that they were missing Little
Red Riding Hood, Cinderella, Hop o' My
Thumb, Santa Claus, and the German Christmas tree. Every town of any size in Germany
possesses, among other institutions of "Kultur," a doll hospital. All the cradle songs and
lullabies, which have more than an ephemeral
life, are born, too, in Germany; also sung
there. It is the paradise on earth of children,
Germany. No child or boy is ever flogged
in a German school. She has no David
Copperfields, no begging children, nor "news-
boys." She has no slums, and her submerged
world is a negligible and diminishing quotient.

A defense of German culture would be
about as senseless an undertaking as an
argument on the advantages of food as a
nutriment. Nevertheless, it will be interest-
ing to contemplate certain features of it at

this time, in their bearing on the war and the present and future state of human evolution. Viewing Culture from a certain angle I suppose God has produced no finer product on this earth than the English gentleman. He is no myth, but a splendid, shining reality, and certainly a model for mankind. The Germans have been the first people of the world to recognize this and endeavor to copy him. There can be no doubt that a large majority of the young British officers who have gone to the front were induced to do so by a chivalrous sense of duty toward their sacrificed ally, Belgium. The spiritual refinement and moral culture of the English gentleman is without equal in this world, in my judgment. This is natural, however, and the logical result of individualism, the spirit of England. Nevertheless, this is a utilitarian age, an economic-bread-and-butter-day, where suppression of self and surrender and immolation to the general good is proved to be the best, not only for the individual, but for the state and for mankind. And this proof exists today in the so-called German "Kultur"; a thing which must be judged or measured by its expression and results.

For example, of 1,000 Russian soldiers in the field, 617 can neither read nor write;

of a like number of Servians, the number of
illiterate is 434; for Belgium, 93 out of 1,000
are illiterate; for France, 30; for England,
10, and for Germany, in order to find an
illiterate soldier there must be 2,000 to draw
from; that is, of the so-called "Huns and
Barbarians," the percentage of illiteracy is
one-fiftieth of one per cent. Illiteracy is
also one of the things *verboten* in Germany;
and its opposite, literacy, is *ueber alles*. No
one has ever heard about the "cultured
classes" in Germany. It is this self-named
group in America and England which is very
worthily seeking to reform and uplift those
not in their order. In Germany the vast
industrial class attends to this itself. The
effective temperance movements spring from
the trade and labor organizations. They
make their own night schools. They claim
and forward the legislation calculated for the
good of the workers in all classes.

The socialists of Germany, composed largely
of the foregoing group, have a matter of 5,000
local societies in the various centers of the
Empire. They publish ninety daily, and
several weekly newspapers, as well as a
number of monthly magazines. The combined circulation of these socialist papers
numbers nearly 2,000,000 daily, with advertis-

ing and subscription returns of nearly $5,000,000 a year. The principal organ of the socialists, "Vorwaerts," has a circulation of 200,000 daily.

Now, whether we have any interest in socialism or not, or whether we understand or believe in it, makes no difference. Every intelligent person knows that any political doctrine, be it socialism, republicanism, democracy or progressivism, is a philosophy, or set of principles worked out for state or government administration, and that socialism is peculiarly a proposition embracing modern and reform ideas. So, in this manner, we arrive at a fair conception of one of the principal aspects of German *Kultur*—the solid reading and economic studies of the great majority of the German industrial classes.

The German government has a Minister of Culture. He is the head of the schools of the country, the state and the municipal theatres, as well as the experimental branches of the government mines and research institutions. There are a dozen cities in Germany owning and supporting finer, more artistic, opera houses and theatres than anything that may be found in New York or London. The recently built Opera House at Cassel, a town of 150,000 people, cost $1,250,000, and has been pronounced a much more beautiful and suitable structure for the purpose than the Opera House at Paris. It is certainly ahead of anything in the United States or England. Small towns of twenty-five or fifty thousand inhabitants possess municipal theatres that would put the playhouses of New York and Chicago to shame. These state and municipal theatres are a part of the *Kultur* and educational system of Germany. They are controlled to a certain extent by the Minister of Culture. Shakespeare for the classic, Ibsen and Maeterlinck for the modern, are played more often, and consequently find greater appreciation in Germany than in England, or Scandinavia, or elsewhere. In fact, there will be more Shakespearian reproduction in a town like Hanover than in the city of London. The scheme, of course, of state and municipal theatres is to keep the taste of the people on a bit higher plane than our vaudevilles and the music halls of England afford, and the best plays and grand operas may be seen and heard for from ten cents to two dollars, according to the purse of the attendant.

It surely is superfluous to touch upon the subject of music as an evidence of German

culture. Nearly all the great composers and
masters of history were German. They have
embraced the whole field of music with but
one exception, and that has been our synco-
pated American rag. The superiority of the
Salvation Army street music in England must
be acknowledged, likewise. It is undoubtedly
the best of its kind in the world. In Sheffield,
the center of the British musical world, the
Citadel Band competes with the Coldstream
Guards for public concerts.

The merest outline of German culture, that
is to say, culture of a German origin, would
alone require many volumes. That she reigns
supreme in the intellectual world is a universal
acknowledgment, and this credit cannot now
be taken from her, even though she is engaged
with those same intellectual forces in the
most terrific and disastrous war any one has
ever dreamed of.

Indeed, the solidarity of the German people,
apparent in the present war, is an evidence of
how thoroughly their institutions have impressed them. All of her forces, intellectual,
spiritual, financial and physical, are formed
into the most absolute unity at this time.
Her seventy million people are as one, let
there be no mistake, as ONE individual, in
the war. Her scientists, philosophers and

teachers are for it to a man. Her musicians, artists, authors and composers are in the trenches. Her priests and churches have unanimously blessed it. Her money is back of it to the final Pfennig. They regard the war as a struggle for the promotion of their civilization and culture, and to them, more than ever to Islam, their war is a holy one.

Every child in the German schools was requested by their teacher to prepare a Christmas box for the soldiers just before the holidays. These boxes were to contain a few sweets, some cakes, cigars and cigarettes— but particularly a letter from the donor to the unknown warrior who might receive it in the trenches. There is a bit of German system serving at once to render a sentimental moral encouragement to the men at the front and at the same time open an opportunity for even the children to participate in the war of the Fatherland. While America was sending Christmas ships to the children of Europe, including Germany, of course, literally millions of Hansels and Gretels, of Fritzes and Irmas, were preparing their gifts *für die tapfere Soldaten* in the field. And when the German arms are more than usually successful the church bells peal from

one end of the empire to the other, the cities
and villages are decorated with flags, and the
schools are given a half holiday, after—
always after—the children have sung their
national songs, "Die Wacht Am Rhein"
and "Deutschland, Deutschland, Ueber
Alles."

These are the children, indeed, of Gutenberg, Kepler and Kant, the future Beethovens,
Mozarts and Wagners of the world. They are
the young Haeckels, Hegels, Fichtes, Goethes,
Schillers and Hauptmanns of science, philosophy and music. They are the Paul Ehrlichs
and Robert Koches, the Mergenthalers, Froe-
bels and Frauenhoefers (who brought the sun
down to the earth through the spectrum) of
tomorrow. German culture is not confined
to the universities, the laboratories, nor to
Weimar, Dresden and Beyreuth. It is everywhere evident in her beautiful and model
cities, in her forests and fields, her modernized
and sanitary workshops and factories—in the
fitness of her people for labor and usefulness.
The Kaiser is a bookbinder by trade, the
crown prince is a carpenter.

According to Professor Cooley of Chicago,
the Kingdom of Prussia contains approxi-
mately three million boys between the ages
of fourteen and sixteen. Some two millions

of these are at work. They quit school and go to work for the same reason that the American boy leaves his school books on the completion of his grammar grade—to become a breadwinner and get a start in life. But when the American boy leaves school that is pretty much the end of it. The state gives his education no further thought. German culture demands a different system than this for its boys. When a boy between the ages of fourteen and eighteen leaves school to take a job, or learn a trade, he still has open to him a large number of vocational schools where he spends one or two days a week continuing his culture or general education in the technique of his chosen trade. The city of Munich, with a population of say half a million, supports over fifty such vocational or continuation schools.

Much has been said of an absence of initiative in the German owing to his surrender to the state. Nothing is less true than this. Perhaps one of the most distinct evidences of initiative is that of invention. In my career as Consul, at Hanover, a city of some industrial importance in Germany, and at Sheffield, an English industrial center of world-wide importance, the consular records

will show not less than five American patent
applications submitted by German inventors
in the Hanover district, as against one in the
Sheffield district. My remembrance is that
the ratio was as ten to one. I place it con-
servatively at five to one. Every man of
the thousands of German soldiers today
bearing the Iron Cross has a story of individual initiative to tell. The Germans possess
initiative plus, more than any people I have
ever seen. Frank Putnam, a brilliant student
of sociology, says:

"Their initiative and culture has lifted
them irresistibly upward through an adaman-
tine crust of political officialdom toward a
full measure of workable, personal liberty.
It has substituted for the age-old scholastic
servitude of modern minds to Greek and
Latin classics, the universal, shrewd and
thorough study of the earth we live on and
the life of the present and tomorrow. It is
giving effect, in the equitable distribution of
material wealth and all that stands for, to the
mighty visions of the poets and philosophers
of the classic age of the German people. It
has produced a people who stand and walk
erect, almost without exception, who breathe
deeply, who dress neatly, work long and
steadily, and live with wise economy, and

who front life with supreme confidence in the future of their nation."

It is German initiative and culture that has made her cities wonders of artistic and cleanly beauty, which attract increasing multitudes of visitors, residents and students from every part of the world. It has given the city of Berlin more square yards of asphalt than any other civic center on the earth. It has excited thousands of inventions and improvements in applied science. It has placed Germany to the forefront of the nations of the earth, in the solution of those intra-social problems which seem to be the special purpose and object of organized society. It has brought her away from and above the entanglements of political government, as understood by the American mind. It has accepted the solution of the questions of human and political rights, and gone on to the practical problems of learning how to live and make the most of life. While the American and English politician and leader is fighting the windmills of the Rights of Man, the Crosses of Gold, and Crowns of Thorns, the German, with really as great a degree of personal liberty as any of us, has turned his face to the sun and is lifting, lifting himself and his state higher and higher among the galaxy of successful peoples of the world to the position of Supernation.

I have the honor to be, Sir,

Your obedient servant,

ROBERT J. THOMPSON,
American Consul (Resigned).

ATROCITIES ON THE FIELD AND
IN THE PRESS

AMERICAN CONSULATE,
AIX–LA–CHAPELLE, GERMANY.

To the Honorable,
The Secretary of State,
Washington, D. C.

Sir:—

I have the honor to submit the following
report touching on the subject of reprisals
in the war zone of Western Europe:

One of the most remarkable things about
the present war is the fact that practically
every disinterested, thinking neutral, who has
come into contact with the German military,
either in Germany, Belgium, or France, even
though ignorant of German ideals or institutions, and prejudiced against her through
this ignorance, has needed but a few hours,
or at most, a few days, to reverse his judgment and conviction more or less completely.
Undoubtedly there are exceptions to this
statement, but I myself know not a single
one and I have had the privilege of meeting

many persons under these circumstances. Calumny, even though permissible on the part of a belligerent, is the meanest, and one of the most effective, weapons in warfare.

Strange enough the neutral commission which goes out to report on alleged brutalities and atrocities on the termination of a war, never or seldom sends a report. There were a number of such commissions sent from Europe to investigate the charges made against the Bulgars and the Turks at the close of the Balkan War. Their reports are still uncompleted. The same may be said of South Africa and the Boer War, and, to a very large extent, you may be sure this will be the case with respect to the conduct of the German troops, and, I dare say, the Russians and French as well.

Many of my friends in England have asked me to explain to them the origin of the reported bitterness and hatred of the Germans for England. It is this—the facility with which England has smirched the German character, from that of the Kaiser to the meanest trooper, in the eyes of the world, and especially in the eyes of those who would normally be in sympathy with him, by its prolific atrocity, brutality and bestiality stories. I am convinced that the fiery resent-

ment of the German toward England is more
the result of this systematic, all-embracing
world-campaign of mendacity and calumny,
even than the awful fact of her rushing in to
brain and destroy him at the moment when
he is engaged in a life and death struggle
with the Russian colossus straining to gar-
rote him from the rear, with France, keen,
purposeful and expert, seeking to rapier him
from the front. Indeed, it cannot be long
before the world, before America, will see and
appreciate the heroic, if not superhuman,
effort Germany is making for its life against
this deluge and hurricane of foes.

I suppose no two journalists in America are
more respected and trusted than John T.
McCutcheon and Irving S. Cobb. These two
gentlemen, in company with James O'Donnell
Bennett, Roger Lewis and Harry Hansen,
representing, respectively, the Chicago
Tribune, Associated Press and the Chicago
Daily News, were pushed into Germany
rather unceremoniously, and as semi-suspects,
along about the end of August. They all had
a grievance against Germany, more or less,
for the treatment they have experienced at
the hands of the German military authorities
in Belgium. Their complaint, however, was
professional and not personal. They felt

that they were bottled and were afraid they could neither get out of Germany themselves, nor be able to send reports off to their papers. Cobb appeared in Aix-la-Chapelle in a butcher's leather jumper, and a pair of felt slippers. He is not a handsome man even when seen on Fifth Avenue; but when he came into the Consulate, unshaved and unwashed, for a period of ten days, he was cursing everything German from the Kaiser to the ordinary "Kannonenfutter," and he looked like a Bavarian charcoal burner. Lewis had left $900 in gold in an open suit case in the Palais Hotel in Brussels. Hansen had been on his honeymoon trip and did not know if his wife was in England or Germany. Bennett and McCutcheon were feverish in their desire to get to London. They had all left England some three weeks before to strike the trail of the Red Terror, and were on the scent of the "mad dog" of Europe.

If these colorful details seem rather paltry and trivial to introduce here, I present them as a simple preface to the very rapid conviction these gentlemen arrived at respecting Germany and her military activities—in Belgium particularly, after witnessing them, individually. Notwithstanding personal grievance, because of deprivation, discomfort and

interference by German army authorities,
they retained their birthright, as real, open-
minded, fair-play Americans; and, as soon
as they compared notes and found all of their
experience alike, they got together, alone in
their room at their hotel, and wrote as briefly
and as tersely as they could a joint statement
refuting the English, French and Belgian
circulated atrocity stories that were filling
the columns of the press of the world. You
will recall that I reported their experiences
in some detail to you in a previous despatch.
Their statement follows:

"Western Union, New York, for *Associated
Press*, signed Lewis; *Ledger*, Philadelphia,
Cobb; *News*, Chicago, Hansen; *Tribune*,
Chicago, Bennett, McCutcheon. In spirit
fairness we unite in declaring German atrocities groundless as far as we are able to observe.
After spending two weeks with the German
army, accompanying troops upward hundred
miles, we unable to report single instance
unprovoked reprisal. Also unable confirm
rumors mistreatment prisoners or non-combatants. With German columns: Lande,
Louvain, Brussels, Nivelles, Binche, Buissiere,
Hautes-Wiherie, Merbes-le-Chateau, Solre-
sur-Sambre, Beaumont, without substantiat-
ing single case wanton brutality.

"Numerous investigated rumors proved groundless. Everywhere have seen German paying for purchases, respecting property-rights of individuals, according civilians consideration.

"After battle Buissiere found Belgian women, children moving comfortably about, day after Germans captured town.

"In Merbes-le-Chateau we found one citizen killed, but unable confirm lack provocation.

"Refugees with tales atrocities unable supply direct evidence.

"Belgian Burgomaster Solre-sur-Sambre voluntarily discounted reports cruelty in surrounding country.

"Discipline German soldiers excellent as observed. No drunkenness.

"To truth these statements we pledge professional, personal word. Please repeat back last three words, care American Consul, Vaals, Holland."

These gentlemen were not of the refugee crowd that rushed out of Belgium into England and France and Holland ahead of the invading forces of Germany. They were left behind; and none of those neutrals who remained on the field, at least none I have met, have, as yet, been able to confirm the hysterical and irresponsible stories of atrocities sent out of London. Donald Thompson, the Kansas war photographer of the New York *World*, who was arrested a dozen times by the German military authorities, wounded once by shrapnel, and present in thirty odd engagements, covering pretty much all of Western Belgium, said to me that he learned of no single case of brutality or unprovoked reprisal on the part of the German troops. This man was being paid a large sum of money, both by the New York *World* and the London *Daily Mail* for war photographs, and atrocity stories, as well as pictures, were at a premium. The baby with its hands cut off, and the nurse with amputated breasts were always in the town or villages just ahead of him, until, finally, these two particular atrocities reached London, in violation of all pathological laws of strangulation and bleeding to death. They have been sought for religiously by many and Bernard Shaw, who spent much time endeavoring to locate them, says that when he was finally told they had gone on to Archangel by way of the

Note.—Since arriving in America I have met a wide-eyed guileless English lady, with the very truth shining from her face, who has assured me that this particular atrocity—the baby with its hands cut off—was living with her own mother near Blackpool, England; and a French friend with whom I have even had business relations for a period of three years tells me the child is with his aunt in Winnipeg. I am certain they both believe what they say.

Arctic Sea, he was compelled to abandon the search.

I have spent much time myself in seeking for German soldiers alleged to have been mutilated, and atrocitied by the Belgian populace. They, too, were not to be found, certainly not by me, and of the members of the Medical Association of the West Rhine Province, which met in Aix-la-Chapelle in October, I could find none who had personal knowledge of such cases. Undoubtedly most savage severities were applied on both sides and all sides, but these things cannot enter into the merits of this great struggle as a determining factor in the judgment of neutral people. War itself is the great atrocity and that is enough, God knows. The man, or men, whom history will make responsible for this war will also be responsible for Belgium. Lord Roberts raised the one sane voice against the atrocity campaign in England. He said: "Let us not forget our concentration camps and raids of fire in South Africa and what the world said about that. We have only to fight the Germans in such a way that, win or lose, they will respect us when the war is over."

The nurse-with-her-breast-cut-off-by-German-soldiers' story originated in Edinboro, and the girl who concocted it has since been convicted by the courts of that good town. The sentence should have included a goodly number of London editors and American correspondents; but, unfortunately for the peace of mind of the world, the court fell short of convicting, for libel, of the perpetrators of the alleged crime, but rendered judgment because of the grief the girl had caused the parents of the mistreated nurse, who, strange enough, was her own sister.

England is the home of melodrama, and in view of this, and the demands of the newspaper reading public, the cheap theatre, music hall, and football millions for that kind of matter, which, to the shame of the British censor, was allowed to go uncut, the judging world must look elsewhere for the truth.

I repeat, the blue-eyed Saxon, the proud Prussian and the German people, all hate the English more for this campaign than if they were to whip them back across Belgium and the Rhine. The German officers and soldiers at the front, have only praise for the English troops for their bravery and fairness on the field of battle.

My friend, Mr. C. H. Wheeler, of the Chicago *Tribune*, came to Europe for the purpose of fetching a thousand Belgian orphans, the harvest of the German invasion, back to open homes in America. The number was fairly modest, considering the tales of the London press and correspondents. That there were no orphans to be had, makes no difference. The world keeps merrily on devouring these noble tales of the sensation mongers of newspaper row in London. Had Mr. Wheeler gone to the East End of London, to Sheffield, Manchester, Leeds, and a few other places in England he could have brought back 10,000 waifs, victims of what may more rightly be considered the present real atrocity of the world—British industrial conditions. I proposed this to Mr. Wheeler at the time, but he said the American people would be satisfied only with war orphans— from Belgium.

Even now you see neither hungry nor freezing children in Belgium—you see many of them in Britain. There is no German Landwehr man who would not divide his last crust and ration with a Belgian woman or child. Under the German social system hunger and unclothed children do not exist. That also is *verboten*. But if there were starving and suffering children in Belgium the condition might fairly be attributed to a state of 'war. In England that condition is the regular, unnoticed horror of Peace. Calloused against her own inability to correct these evils, deaf to the cries of those who wish to draw her out of the awful slough of administrative impotence, she points her finger toward the Germans and prints, in her great illustrated papers, faked pictures of them carrying Belgian babies on bloody lances.

This is the moral warfare of England, with her world cables, her world mails, and her practically universal language. This is the chivalry of warfare her Conan Doyles, Arnold Bennetts and H. G. Wells' write about, on which they make plea for American sympathy. And it is disgusting and unworthy of a great people. It is because of the foregoing facts, partly, that I feel that the American people have been stampeded in their conviction and sympathies. The war will continue long enough for the world to cool off and anathematize the real offenders—long enough for a readjustment of sympathies and sentiment—at least such as may have been based upon the "Atrocities."

It was as sure and easy for England and the Allies to capture the favorable sentiment of the world, they having the cables, mails

and press for the moment, as it was for
Germany, with her military preparedness to
throw the sphere of operations into the
territory of her opponents. The "Atrocity"
guns and "Militarism" mortars of the Allies'
press have been more effective, indeed, on
this side of the Atlantic, than the Krupp 42's
in Belgium and France.

Some weeks ago the London *Graphic*
printed a double page picture of a score or
more of bridges destroyed along the river
Meuse, with the caption: "The work of the
German army in Belgium." The facts were
that the Belgian and French pioneers had
blown up every bridge from near Aix-la-
Chapelle, on the German frontier, clear up
the river as far as Verdun, in France, and
not less than a hundred of them have been
partially, if not completely, restored, already,
by the German army. Military necessity

Editor's Note.—Mr. Thompson writes us: "Since arriving in
America I have listened to one of Mr. Elmendorf's travel lectures,
during which that gentleman threw several pictures of Liege on the
screen. Amongst them was a view of the University building. Mr.
Elmendorf remarked that this, along with the other buildings shown
were totally destroyed. This is not at all true. They are untouched
excepting for a few window panes which were broken by bullets in
the University building. I slept in that building on the twenty-
eighth of August, and visited it later, the fourth of October, 1914.
The destruction of buildings in Liege would not equal in loss the
amount of a fair-sized fire in Chicago, such as causes public comment
for two or three days only. This is mentioned merely to indicate
the unconscious dissemination of exaggerated and false statements
by presumed authorities.

constructs as well as destroys, but such
statements make good moral shrapnel against
the sons of the Kaiser, and so we have to take
it, requiring as we do, news and war pictures.

The moral responsibility for the desecration
and destruction of churches would be difficult
to place. It is certain that where engagements
or battles did not take place the churches are
intact, and in good shape. I have photo-
graphed German soldiers at prayer in these
same churches, and witnessed the Kaiser
participating in the services. But where they
did take place in towns or cities the place at
once and automatically became a citadel and
fort under military law and the highest point
of vantage for observation and signaling was
invariably the church, whether it was a
thousand years old, and decorated with
masterpieces of Rubens and Van Dyke, or
six months old, and plastered with machine-
made statuary from Neuilly, Paris.

Obviously, if a people purposed to save its
churches from an attacking army, they should
exercise as much intelligence, at least, as the
partridge, which instinctively seeks to beguile
the hound away from its nest. France took
her churches away from God some few years
ago and added them to the list of government
property; and, anyway, God doesn't seem to

be much concerned with the present war;
for the good people of Belgium, France,
England, Russia, Germany and Austria, and,
I doubt not, Servia and Turkey, are holding
simultaneous intercessionals to Him for success in killing their Christian neighbors.
I am sure, if what General Von Zweel, com-
manding the German forces before Rheims,
told me was true, that the French were
observed signaling their artillery from the
cathedral tower, and that he sent several
parley emissaries to warn them, without
effect, then the desecration was first committed by our French friends, and they were
alone responsible for forcing the bombard-
ment. I think it is fair to say they were the
inciting cause. My observation during the
past several years has been that the "Hun"
has as much respect for churches, generally,
as the "Frank."

I have the honor to be, Sir,

Your obedient servant,

ROBERT J. THOMPSON,
American Consul (Resigned).

THE BLOOD OF AMERICA

AMERICAN CONSULATE,
AIX–LA–CHAPELLE, GERMANY.

To THE HONORABLE,
  THE SECRETARY OF STATE,
    WASHINGTON, D. C.

Sir:—

I have the honor to submit the following studies on the subject of the "Blood of America," and the part contributed thereto by the German:

The contribution of Germany to that marvelous composite which forms the American has been great almost beyond calculation, but not of modern Germany, that Germany we see today fighting for the results of her new national life. The hordes of German immigrants that passed through the broad and open gateways of America in the earlier days have long since dwindled to trickling streams of relatives of the composite American and to artists, scientists, and commercial representatives. Out of that older supply of German blood, and running into the

second, third, fourth generation, etc., there
should be no less than twenty-five million
souls in the United States, who spring through
direct, or indirect descent, from full or mixed
German parentage. It may be truthfully
said that this enormous and much mixed
element in our blood has never, heretofore,
had occasion to express itself as a solidarity
with but a few local and insignificant exceptions. The German immigrant to America
sprang almost entirely from the humbler,
more ignorant peasant population of the
various kingdoms, principalities, etc., of the
old defunct German confederation. They
came as refugees from apparently hopeless
political and economic conditions, and they
were absorbed by millions into this composite
body. Beyond the second generation little
is left to distinguish their origin besides the
name and possibly present harking back in
sentiment to the vine and fig tree of the
Fatherland.

In the year 1750 there were, in the colony
of Pennsylvania, over fifty thousand German
residents and settlers. Now, according to
the rule used by statisticians, in estimating
the growth of population, in a new and
progressive country, these figures may be
doubled for each twenty-five years. On this

basis there would be, at the present time, over five million Germans, or persons of full German blood in or coming from the state of Pennsylvania alone. It happens that in this instance we have figures of an early date. The question was at that time discussed in the Pennsylvania colonial assembly as to whether the proceedings of that body should not be conducted in the German language. It was shortly after this that the Mecklenburg declaration of independence was issued by German patriots, at Charlotte, North Carolina. This antedated the Philadelphia declaration by one year. Up to 1871, no proper record was kept by the United States Government of immigration, but the largest immigration we have ever had came to us from Germany. And based upon more or less actual figures, a fair estimate is reached of the astounding fact that nearly one-third of the white blood of America is today purely Germanic; one-quarter Celtic, one-eighth Scandinavian, a considerable percentage of Dutch, Italian, French, Spanish and Russian, and finally about one-eighth of what we call, in the commonly accepted sense of the term, Anglo-Saxon.

It is true, and possibly fortunate, for us, that we are possessed today of English laws,

language and institutions, generally, a fact
due to the control of the colonial governments, courts, schools and other institutions,
by England. Interwoven into the history
and growth of the country, like threads of
gold, are the names of Washington, Jefferson,
Hamilton, the Adamses, Jackson, Fremont,
Lincoln, Lee, etc. But when the tie between
England and the colonies was finally severed
in 1790, a new race and blood product was
born into the world. It is a myth, a legend
and a mistake to look upon England as the
mother country. The American people are,
in the matter of purely blood relationship to
Europe, less English than they are Scandinavian, and more German than anything else.
Nevertheless, our impetus, or progress and
civic development, was received from this,
at the time, leading nation of the world,
England, and what we have of good, as well
as evil, we have largely from her. Our much
praised political freedom, along with our
unemployed; our opportunities for success
and advantage as an individual, parallel with
the muddling, inefficient effort to advance
the general welfare; our immense success in
spots, and lamentable failures in other direc-
tions; these are the results of national ideals
inherited from England. There is something

new in this respect, however, in the world, and if we, like England, close our eyes to it, much the worse for us, as it may be for her.

It seems for Germany that God endowed this particular part of the world with an indigenous atmosphere of human fecundity, a fact which has enabled the Germans to send out streams of life to all parts of the earth, and to increase their population, even now at home, more rapidly than any similar number of people anywhere. This, of course, refers only to increase by native birth. In those primitive days, when, according to Gibbon, the German forests were teeming with barbarians, the Angles occupied Briton, the Franks and Burgundians, Gaul, the Lombards, Upper Italy, and later the millions to America, to Brazil, Australia, Africa and Asia; all proving that one of the characteristics of the Germans has ever been the so-called "Wanderlust." *"Aus aus in die weite, weite Welt, dort wo du nicht bist, dort ist das Gluck."*

Up to 1870 the German had no real nationality. He was a poet, a philosopher, or a soldier, peculiarly adapted to absorption wherever he might find himself. But today all is changed under the inspiration and guidance of one of the dominating great

masters of men, and by one of those phe-
nomenally rare processes of nature, he arises
a rejuvenated race. The gods have given
Germany a new youth. That great *Drang
nach Aussen*, that age old, pathetic and never
dying *Wanderlust*, which for centuries resulted
only in the building up of other lands, has at
last been dammed, and from this great and
inexhaustible reservoir of enterprise she has
launched a thousand ships and forces, directed
to the uttermost parts of the earth for the
occupation thereof, as a World Power and
economic entity.

With a scientific and purely business-like
administration of the affairs of the people,
where duty is the first consideration of citizen-
ship and "rights" a proper second, she stands
today, after a brief career of forty years, the
most brilliant and unparalleled example of
the effectiveness of government, so-called,
perhaps in the history of man.

It appears to me that Germany is organized
on the principle of the people being the stock-
holders, and the government the board of
directors, of a great industrial concern. The
question of government, in its ethical sense,
resolving itself into a matter of the direction
and control of the natural resources and
productive forces of the country for the

greatest good of all, with the overworked
shibboleth of the rights of man, solved,
practically a century ago, being left to the
academician and demagogue, while real Germany, with her modern team-work and
practical applications of socialism—not to
forget her administration by trained and
specialized experts—has quietly and surely
stepped into the lead amongst the nations of
the earth.

The ideals of man today are economic, and
Germany is astride, armed cap-a-pie, of this
supreme fact of modern life. Her savings,
through the investments of industrial insurance funds, already form the treasure of a
nation. Over twenty million workers stand
under the mantel of this protection with
resources of more than three billion of dollars.
If her canals and navigable rivers were given
to the United States in like proportion, as
regards length of water courses and area of
land, they would extend in twenty parallel
lines across the continent from the Atlantic
to the Pacific and in forty parallel lines from
Canada to the Gulf of Mexico. There is a
greater freight tonnage on the river Rhine
alone than on all our great lake system. Her
prosperity and material progress are such
that she must employ some three millions

of female workers in the fields to garner the harvests, so plentiful through intensive and scientific cultivation, an element in her life that contributes enormously to the health and virility of the race. I might enumerate a hundred of things, like the German marine, education, chambers of commerce, railroads, municipal improvements—I could speak of these things and many others, and they would show but the modern and up-to-date organization as a really new force in the world—a state administered on business principles, and a state, not old, but one just entering upon and at the commencement of the fruition of successful achievement. Germany may be defeated in war but she is already the victor in the real rivalry of the states of the world in peaceful competition.

I have the honor to be, Sir,

Your obedient servant,

ROBERT J. THOMPSON,
American Consul (Resigned).

THE ATTITUDE AND DUTY OF AMERICA

AMERICAN CONSULATE,
AIX–LA–CHAPELLE, GERMANY.

To the Honorable,
The Secretary of State,
Washington, D. C.

Sir:—

I have the honor to suggest for the consideration of the Department the following proposals respecting the attitude and duty of our government in relation to the present war in Europe.

A suspended judgment on the war is the important thing for America. Difficult as this may be, under the circumstances, it is the one great desideratum for the United States. The coincidental fact that coupled with a preponderating sentiment of the American people against the German, there exists likewise a condition which makes us a large and powerful contributor to the forces of his opponents, possibly even to becoming the determining factor in the outcome of the conflict, makes it doubly incumbent upon us to exercise great caution in taking a positive position, lest we be unfair.

The various Foreign Offices of Europe make out their cases under the published title of the White, Yellow, or some other Book of this or that country. Each proves its own contention, that the immediate, if not entire, responsibility for the opening of hostilities rests upon the other party. We take our choice, perhaps, according to our instincts, sympathies, prejudices, or, if possessed of average fairness of mind, following such information as we may obtain, be it interested, or disinterested. The following expression is cited as illustrating the American's attitude of neutrality: "Sure I'm perfectly neutral, I don't care which nation licks Germany!" Now the fact that the German, as an individual, is more of a personal favorite with the American than is the Englishman, would indicate that our position is not predicated on favoritism or purely sentimental inclination.

The thought exists very generally throughout America that Germany precipitated the war, or that, if she did not do that, she, at least, was in a position to prevent it. That may be true or not, but the same claim may be made of Austria, Russia, France or England. There is little doubt that any of those five powers could have checked hostilities, if, indeed, not even prevented them, altogether. It seems that both Germany and England did try this. My conviction is that neither of these powers desired war, though a successful war offered advantages to both of them—to England in the maintenance of her foremost place as a World Power, and to Germany as a release from the pressure and restrictions being put upon her by the Entente.

However, the chief question now for the United States is what we can do to prepare ourselves for and to aid in bringing about peace, and a peace that cannot again be easily disturbed. It is not impossible that the eventual decision of this war may lie with us. Owing to our wealth, power, and advanced place as a world force, we should automatically come to the position of final peacemaker and arbiter of the nations at war. If this be true, it is of transcendant importance that we have a clear national vision and comprehension of the fundamental causes and events of the war, unaffected by prejudices, sympathies or misinformation.

It will be of no avail, nor lead to any real solution to point to Servia's assassination of

the head of a neighboring state, nor to
Austria's peremptory demands on Servia. It
will not answer to point to the hostile and
threatening mobilization of Russia against
Austria and Germany, and the latter's swift
movement across Belgium to the North Sea,
and France seeking to balance, in a measure,
the tremendous odds forming against her,
by her mobility and preparedness.

All these things will be of no avail. Each
nation is justified in its own conscience for
its action. We must not overlook this.
These people are very highly civilized. They
are all firmly convinced that God and Right
are on their side. Their hearts are full of
human love and honor. They are the victims
of a vast and fatal miscalculation, a system
of international rivalry, and a soulless Machia-
vellian foreign office—of intrigue and barter.
A long, educational, political campaign and
eventual plebiscite must be had for the most
insignificant change in the internal policy
of a nation. Its foreign relations and power
to make war are as much in the hands of one
man, or a small group of men, today, as they
were in the time of Caesar or Peter the Great.
And this is likewise true, though in less
degree, perhaps, of us.

What, then, are we to learn from the war?

What are we to gain? Will the end fix forever the solution of the question of national armament or disarmament?

Shall we be able to learn whether, or no, we must become a part of a great world contest for military power, on sea or land? Whether the gauge of greatness of a people shall really be in their dreadnaughts and land military establishments—whether, in fact, the determination of England to maintain her place as mistress of the sea, or Germany's purpose to remain the chief continental political force have justified, in any way, the great expenditures the world has witnessed, or the enormous loss of life now taking place. If we shall be able to predicate our own future from these present events, that may be worth while to us.

But greater than all may be our opportunity, at this moment, to direct the future course of international ambition and international ideals. In this respect we still occupy the favored position, and should make the most of it. We have a supreme and magnificent duty and work before us; and, according to our real nobleness of mind and foresight, we can perform this duty. How insignificant and paltry, then, must be the attitude of small partisanship. We must,

if necessary, rise above the trammeling level
of so-called international laws, which bind
us, as an unwilling, though neutral, partici-
pant in the war, and drags us along, without voice or power, toward the tremendous
solution of this final problem of the relationship of the nations of the world.

I am told that in the State Department
there was great agitation and apparent con-
fusion on the third and fourth of August of
last year, that the one ray of light and
satisfaction existing there in those fatal
hours was the vista of a great opening for
American business and export trade. Be
this as it may, what an opportunity there
was for Mr. Wilson to then and there have
placed the United States on a plane that
would have made these belligerent friends of
ours to pause and realize there was a force
in the world greater even than their dreadnaughts or Krupp mortars.

The declaration of American neutrality
should have taken the form of an act of
Congress, and it should have been of a character comporting with the bigness of the war
and the issues which may come out of it.
We should have announced, not from the
State Department, but as an expression of
all the people, a super-neutrality. We should

The Attitude and Duty of America   121

have protested against the war to every
nation, and as fast as they became involved,
no matter what their Yellow, White, or Blue
Books might say, we should have withdrawn
our representatives from those countries and
closed our ports entirely to their commerce,
ships and cables. That would have been a
neutrality which would have allowed us to
formulate the future great Peace Pact of the
world. To introduce, when the moment
arrived, the proposal for an international
constitution, or world contract, out of which
would naturally evolve those world courts of
Law and Equity and Arbitration, of which
we have dreamed, and endeavored to promote,
without the foundation—necessary for any
competent court—an existing statutory, international law. The great biological decree
and law of nature, that might is right, is but
another name for International Law, or the
Law of Nations—gloss it over as we may.
The principles and precepts of these hazy
international regulations must ever have,
under present conditions, their final adjudica-
tion at the cannon's mouth. And this is
because each nation interprets the so-called
rules of international law according to its
own particular traditions, prejudices and
interests. A high international court, supreme

in the matter of the relations of one nation
to another, could only be founded upon a
genuine international law, and such international law is not now a fixed institution.
Statutory law is as necessary a precedent to
the formation of a competent court as city
ordinances are to a police court. We can
never, therefore, have such international tri-
bunals as we have been endeavoring to promote at the Hague and elsewhere, until we
first create a real international law, and such
a law must eventually take the form of an
international constitution, or world contract.
Such a contract embodying even the very
first and most primitive rules of international
law, which presumably would be acceptable
to all nations, would be sufficient to automatically create the great need for an interpretation of such rules, in their application
to questions of facts and equity arising between the nations. With such a beginning
the development of an international statute
to meet the problems of relations between
the nations might be assured.

However, we did not rise to the occasion.
We looked backwards fifty, one hundred, a
thousand years for precedents and rules for
a stand that would serve to eliminate us
from a part in this upheaval and readjustment

of the relationship of nations. Mr. Wilson
and you, Mr. Bryan, threw away the opportunity, in this first instance, to lay the
foundation for the much dreamed of and
hoped for federation of the world.

But is it too late, even now, to strive for
this end? I do not think so. In the articles
I have written on the causes and merits of the
controversy, between England and Germany
especially, I have been moved, particularly,
by the wish to show the equities of the situation from the German side, not with the wish
to excite a reversal of American sentiment,
per se, but to prepare the public mind for a
clearer and fairer judgment than it can now
render.

So far as the end of the war is concerned,
there is no indication of it anywhere. Italy
and Roumania are not the solution. Germany is impregnable on her own territory,
and impregnable against the world. Against
her, on the other hand, stands a force apparently impossible of destruction or defeat.
It resolves, itself, therefore, into a proposition in physics—the collision of two irre-
sistible bodies. Now, these are our own
people. What can we do to save them from
themselves and one another? If we wait
until one or the other cries "Enough," we

will wait too long. Dreadnaughts, aeroplanes, submarines and Zeppelins are new elements in warfare. Their great power for destruction demands also new and unusual methods toward peace. Are we to wait until two thousand pound cargoes of nitro-glycerine are dropped on the city of London? I shall be frank and say I am convinced that the Germans hold the trump card in the fight, not in a general way, but through specific knowledge—applied to the means of war, and that, through the demonstration of a superior and more rational civilization than any other state has so far shown, the merits of the contest, so far as this goes, are on her side. But if this, or any other superiority in offence, results in the destruction of England, or France, or of Germany, and we might be the means of preventing it, and did not do all in our power to do so, the fault of omission on our part would be great, if not so great as the crime of commission on the part of any one of the belligerents.

Therefore, I propose that a peace commission be at once formed by Congress, to be composed of our two ex-presidents and three others, who shall be authorized to confer at once with the powers at war with the view of bringing about a cessation of hostilities, and that they

*be further delegated to propose the complete
disarmament at sea and on the land of the
several powers of the world. It will come to this
eventually. Why not rise to the occasion and
prepare for it now?*

In view of this duty, existing now, or ahead
of the United States, it is of supreme importance that, whatever our reason tells us,
as to the virtues of the great controversy, we
check and suppress our sympathies and
prejudices, and refrain from weakening our
position, or making ourselves impossible as
the final forces which shall determine the
direction and course to be taken at the
settlement of the war.

We cannot go back to the ententes and
alliances, to the annexation of Herzegovina
and Bosnia, the assassination of Ferdinand,
the ultimatum of Austria, the mobilization of
Russia, the breach of Belgian neutrality—
we must look solely to the future, and that
future must be an assurance to mankind that
neither Foreign Secretaries, Kings, nor Presi-
dents, may ever again upset the peace of the
world, either through ententes and alliances,
or superiority in armament, on the land, at
sea, or in the air.

There are several conditions in Europe, at
present, we should understand: First, neither

of the chief belligerents are thinking of peace,
and would probably repel any ordinary effort
to introduce the subject. In Germany there
is a supreme and exalted confidence in the
favorable outcome of the war to them. The
same may be said also of the feeling in England. Each one regards it its duty to defeat
the other and does not, as yet, question the
final issue. These conditions we would have
to face. So much greater might be the success
of our efforts.

As to the feeling of the belligerents toward
us, it is simple enough. The Allies know
they have the sympathy at present of the
American people, generally, and they consider this as a great moral, if not material
asset. Germany witnesses the matter with
stoicism, and a recognition of the technical
justification of our position. She has full
confidence in our fairness, and feels only that
she has been misrepresented and misunderstood, and that time will set her right.

Germany does not, nor did she ever wish
to make Belgium a part of German territory.
A treaty of peace such as Germany may dic-
tate to England will probably result in the
restoration to Belgium of her sovereignty—
the repayment to Liege, Brussels and Ant-
werp and her other cities and provinces, of

the war tributes exacted from them, and when the final accounting is made, Germany will not disappoint the world in her generosity to this crushed and unhappy state. She wants no more from Belgium, even now, than she asked of her, as a life and death necessity, on the third of August, at the commencement of the war.

The moral, practical and Christian forces of the United States of America are now being weighed in the balance. Shall we be found wanting? Or shall we rise to this occasion, supreme in our history, and which shall never pass our way again?

I have the honor to be, Sir,

Your obedient servant,

ROBERT J. THOMPSON,
American Consul (Resigned).